I0457072

Invitations to Diplomacy

This series was launched by DiploFoundation in 2018. It aims to provide authors with the opportunity to publish introductory works on any important diplomatic subject, and to make them as accessible as possible in terms of style and costs.

The Diplomacy of Ancient Greece

A Short Introduction

G. R. Berridge

Emeritus Professor of International Politics,
University of Leicester, UK
and
Senior Fellow, DiploFoundation

www.diplomacy.edu

Cover design by: Viktor Mijatovic (DiploFoundation)

ISBN: 979-8-9870052-2-4

Published by: Diplo US (2022)

For Hannah

Contents

Preface   *viii*

List of boxes   *x*

List of maps   *xi*

Introduction   1

1 Personnel   7
   Proxeny   7
   Heralds   11
   Ambassadors   13

2 Bilaterals – private as well as public   21
   Open diplomacy and the art of rhetoric   21
   Private negotiations   22
   Treaties   25

3 Multilaterals   29
   Religious leagues   29
   Military alliances   31
   Interstate arbitration   35
   Panhellenic public festivals   38

4 Conclusion: Were the diplomatic methods of the ancient Greeks 'fit for purpose'?   42

Some important dates   46

References   48

Preface

This brief introduction to the diplomacy of ancient Greece was originally drafted as a chapter for a book that many years ago I planned to write with John W. Young; we proposed to call this 'A History of Diplomacy'. Unfortunately, because of more urgent priorities we both came to realise that we lacked the time to complete it. But it seemed a shame simply to cast aside the chapter I had written, the more so since the only other general treatment of its subject, *Diplomacy in Ancient Greece* (1975) by Sir Frank Adcock and D. J. Mosley, while quite accessible and still immensely valuable, has a rather awkward structure and no maps; furthermore, much valuable work on the subject, not least on proxeny by William Mack, has been produced since their book was published over 40 years ago. When, therefore, the opportunity to publish my draft presented itself, I jumped at it. At first I thought simply to refresh it here and there and provide some illustrations, but as I came to grips with the subject once more I discovered many weaknesses in my draft. As a result, I have revised it extensively and produced a work double its original length.

I am not an ancient historian, although I have published one piece on the diplomacy of the ancient Near East: 'Amarna diplomacy: a fully-fledged diplomatic system?', in R. Cohen and R. Westbrook (eds), *Amarna Diplomacy: The Beginnings of International Relations* (Johns Hopkins University Press, Baltimore, 2000). Nor do I read Greek. There is in consequence no original research in this book. I have certainly gone back to translations of some of the most important primary sources, notably Herodotus, Thucydides, Xenophon, Plutarch, Diodorus the Sicilian, Isocrates, and the speeches of Demosthenes and Aeschines. But this book is essentially a work of synthesis of existing scholarship designed for the student of diplomacy with no prior knowledge of the subject, as well as for the general reader.

To avoid over-cluttering the pages, as a rule I have restricted the footnotes to parenthetical notes not worthy of highlighting in a box, and to sources for quotations and statements that might otherwise raise an eyebrow. The list of references at the end of each chapter is designed not just as a guide to further reading but also to indicate on which works I have relied most heavily. The 'References' in the endmatter provides a complete list of works on which I have drawn.

There have been 11 translations of Thucydides' indispensable history of the Peloponnesian War, which by most accounts is virtually untranslatable. I have used my old copy of the Rex Warner translation, first published by Penguin Books in 1954.

However, I recommend as the most accessible version for students the Landmark reprint of Richard Crawley's 1866 translation, edited by Robert Strassler (see Liz Crawley's piece in *The Oxonian Review* [www]). For those who prefer to read online, the same translation is used in the excellent Perseus Digital Library (in which where available I also cite translations of other important ancient texts). Where I cite Thucydides in the footnotes, I use the page numbers from the Penguin edition but, to ease their discovery in the Crawley translations or any others, I add in square brackets the conventional referencing for such works, e.g. 'pp. 113-14 [2.29.1]', the latter meaning Book 2, Chapter 29, Section 1.

The maps in this book are all reproduced from the 'Atlas of Greece', a part of the Wikimedia Commons Atlas of the World' [www]

The focus of this book is almost entirely on what modern scholars call the 'Classical' period of ancient Greek history, which corresponds roughly to the fifth and fourth centuries BCE (Before the Common Era). Except where otherwise indicated, dates in the text are BCE.

As in earlier editions, I have avoided providing URLs for online sources, partly because they are often so long, partly because they tend to change or disappear, and partly because it is usually easy enough to find a web resource via a search engine; I simply add '[www]' to a reference available on the Internet at the time of writing, although a few might be behind paywalls.

I am grateful to John W. Young for his encouraging remarks on an early draft, and to Hannah Slavik and Mina Mudric of DiploFoundation for supporting the launch of the book.

G. R. B., *Leicester, December 2018*

List of boxes

Box 1.1	Demosthenes, 384-322	9
Box 1.2	Aeschines, 389-314	9
Box 1.3	Nicias, c. 470-414/13	16
Box 1.4	Corinth: centre of trade – and foreign intelligence	18
Box 2.1	Personal friendship and private negotiations	23
Box 3.1	The Delphic Amphictyony	31
Box 3.2	The Decree of Aristoteles, 377	34
Box 3.3	The Melitaea-Narthakion arbitration, ca. 143: a multistate tribunal	36

List of maps

Greek dialects: geographical distribution during the Classical period   2

The Greek states at the outbreak of the Peloponnesian War, 431   8

The Peloponnesian War   12

The main sanctuaries of Classical Greece   30

The Delian League ('Athenian Empire') in 431   33

Introduction

War is often said to have been the hallmark of the relations between the cities of ancient Greece but diplomacy had more than a walk-on part. This is because, as in the Italian peninsula in the late fifteenth century AD, a minimum recognition of common interests by numerous armed political entities existed alongside a shared culture and means of communication adequate to the geography of the region. In short, diplomacy was possible and acknowledged to be needed.

The character of these conditions, which included the attitude of the Greeks to political life in general, gave their diplomacy a particular shape and flavour. How were the city-states – for such was the nature of their armed political entities – represented abroad? In other words, who were their diplomats, what tasks were they given, and how did they conduct themselves? Why was the style of their negotiations unusual by modern standards? What role was played by multilateral diplomacy in ancient Greece? Finally, how *effective* were its diplomatic reflexes? These are the chief questions to which the following pages will suggest answers.

The ancient Greek world had over a 1000 city-states (*poleis*, singular *polis*), which made them the components of 'the most densely populated state system in recorded history.'[1] Left at that, this would have militated against a manageable diplomacy: too many conflicts, too many negotiations to conduct simultaneously with the slender resources available. But for long periods many if not most of these small cities were also members of religious leagues and regional federations or confederations such as those of the Boeotians, Achaeans and Aetolians.

Diplomacy, which requires mutual understanding and certain shared assumptions favourable to the amelioration of conflict, was facilitated in ancient Greece by the culture shared by its people; as the historian Herodotus wrote with the war to resist the Persian invasion in the early fifth century in mind, 'we are all Greeks ... with a common way of life.'[2] Differences on methods of government between democratic, oligarchical and monarchical cities, and ethnic rivalries such as those between Dorians and Ionians, certainly sharpened conflicts; but they were not so deep as to present insuperable obstacles to diplomacy, and were no obstacle at all to diplomacy among their own. The Greeks might fight each other, typically over disputed territory, but in contrast to warring with 'barbarians' (non-Greeks), said the Athenian philosopher,

---

[1]   Mack, *Proxeny and Polis*, p. vii.
[2]   Herodotus, *The Histories*, Book 8.144.

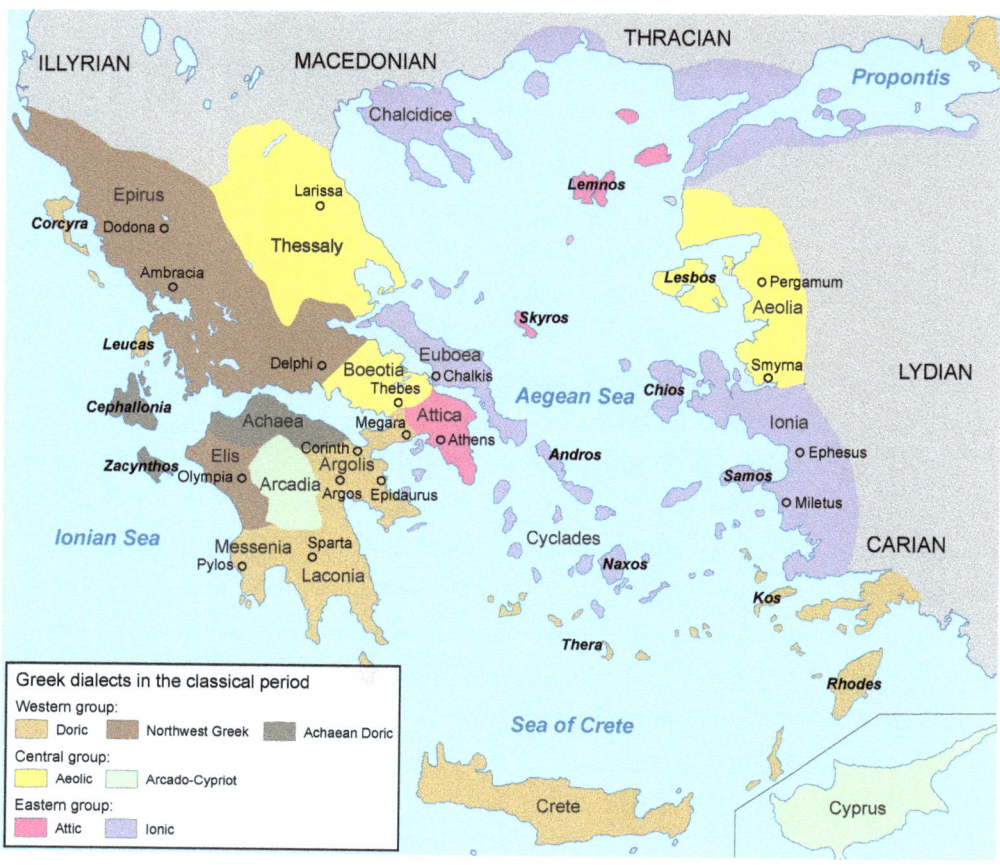

Greek Dialects: Geographical Distribution during the Classical Period

Plato, this was unnatural, fomented by factions, and better regarded as 'civil strife' than 'war'. It was, therefore, to be conducted in a more civilized manner;[3] this made diplomatic reconciliation easier. In any case, more important than their differences were shared religious and other customs, seen most obviously in the great Panhellenic games (see Chapter 3). In addition, there was the 'instinctive love of argument' displayed by the Greeks from earliest times and latterly 'stimulated by the study of rhetoric and philosophy'; to argue from reason is not to fight.[4] To cap their cultural solidarity, the Greeks shared a language. It is true that the country exhibited a bewildering variety

---

[3]   No captured fellow Greeks to be sold into slavery, no gratuitous destruction to be visited on captured territory, and no plundering the corpses of dead soldiers, except for their weapons, Plato, *The Republic*, pp. 227-30 [v. 469-71].

[4]   Westlake, 'Diplomacy in Thucydides', p. 227. Compare the radically different arguments of Nicolson, *Evolution of Diplomatic Method*, p. 10 and Grant, 'A note on the tone of Greek diplomacy'. Both maintain that the intensely competitive spirit of the Greeks and their passion for straight talking and love of altercation was fatal to diplomacy. Besides the glaring omissions in Grant's article, I have read far too many despatches sent home by ambassadors boasting of the strong language they used with local ministers to take too seriously the kind of evidence it adduces. Westlake rightly gives it no more than a polite, passing glance and Nicolson's shallow elegance is routinely ignored by historians of ancient Greece.

of dialects and that the differences between them were quite marked. But as a result of the political, cultural and commercial preponderance of Athens, by the end of the fifth century its own dialect, Attic, had become a common (*koine*) everyday language. When Philip of Macedon made it the official language of his kingdom in the 4th century, it was soon the *lingua franca* of the whole Hellenic world (mainland Greece plus its many colonies). Moreover, it was a language with characteristics well suited to the complex and yet clear argument required by diplomacy.

Diplomacy within ancient Greece and between the city-states and neighbouring regions, especially the Achaemenid Empire of Persia, was also facilitated by means of communication adequate to the purposes of common messengers, heralds and ambassadors. Admittedly, telecommunications, whether acoustic or optical (beacon-chains for example), were virtually useless for diplomatic purposes, being capable of little more than transmitting warnings of danger, or news of the outcome of a battle. It is also true that the country was mountainous and the roads bad or non-existent, so that neither wagons, chariots, nor even horses were in general much use. Such roads as did exist served mainly to facilitate access to the great temples and major festivals; for example, the sacred way from Athens to Eleusis, where the 'mysteries' were regularly celebrated (see Chapter 3). Furthermore, robbers were a risk outside the city walls, and pirates and privateers plagued the open sea, although the latter problem began to abate a little in the sixth century and, at least for the middle years of the fifth century was brought under control by the supremacy of the Athenian fleet. But in any case, geography also provided compensations.

Greece is a small country surrounded by the sea and indented by gulfs and inlets, so most of the city-states were to be found clustered relatively close to its lengthy coastline or on islands in the Aegean or off the coast of Asia Minor.[5] As a result, sea travel was a common option and many of the voyages needed were short; passage by sea was also very cheap and an important message could be sent by a freshly-crewed trireme, a war galley propelled by three banks of oars and capable of speeds of up to nine nautical miles per hour over limited distances. Sea travel also facilitated communication with Persia, since until the time of Alexander the Great this extended to the eastern coast of the Aegean Sea, and the great king's powerful regional governors (satraps) in the coastal provinces conducted much of his diplomacy with the Greeks – and dealt with the Greeks on their own behalf when in rebellion against him. The important city of Sardis, only about 70 kilometres inland from the modern Turkish port of Izmir, connected to the king's far-distant residence of Susa via the 'Royal Road'.

---

[5] Settlements *on* the shoreline had traditionally been regarded as too vulnerable to pirate attacks.

Because most overland journeys in Greece were relatively short, these could be undertaken on foot; indeed, when speed was important, runners were invariably employed, couriers on horseback only occasionally. Writing in the late nineteenth century but in a vein that would have been equally consoling to a traveller in the fifth century, the eminent geographer and classical scholar Henry Tozer remarked that 'the traveller is surprised by the insignificant distances which separate places of world-wide renown.'[6] In sum, while journeying over and around ancient Greece was in general 'neither easy nor particularly pleasant,' it could – except sometimes in deep winter – usually be done relatively quickly.[7] In short, the communications of these centuries did not present a serious obstacle to an active diplomacy. Sometimes it was possible for ambassadors to send messengers home for fresh instructions, or go back themselves and return in time to conclude a vital negotiation, as did the Theban ambassadors at Sparta (the chief settlement of Lacedaemon), where the terms of the settlement of the Corinthian War demanded by the Persian king, Artaxerxes, 'the King's Peace', were accepted by the Greeks in 387.[8]

Thus the existence of the necessary conditions for diplomacy in ancient Greece: a multiplicity of states usually organized into a manageable system of larger units, a shared culture, and adequate communications. What made diplomacy *essential* was that, by definition, among the cities none was so powerful that it could for long hold the rest in thrall. 'As each of the great states in turn – Athens, Sparta, Thebes – attained to a too commanding position,' remarks Tozer, 'a combination was formed amongst the others to put it down.'[9] The principle that operated in Greece as a whole could also be seen in its regions, where a major power such as Sparta in the Peloponnese sometimes provoked an alliance of lesser powers against it. At the other extreme, there was pressure to form Hellenic alliances for the purpose of combating extra-Greek powers – Persia, Macedonia, and finally Rome – and then, as also in the much later case of the Italian city-states, there were always those among the Greeks who wished for outside support in their local squabbles. All such manoeuvres, prompted by an interest in security shared by those in fear of the hegemon, required an energetic diplomacy. In the end, the hegemon had to negotiate as well.

And then there was the widespread, if not common interest in trade. Despite the primitive agricultural economy of the time and the isolated locations of most dwelling places, self-sufficiency in essential commodities was not readily attainable. As a result, facilitated by the surrounding sea and many good harbours, ancient Greece saw

---

[6] Tozer, *Lectures*, p. 4.

[7] Sealey, *Demosthenes*, p. 152. On travelling as 'part of the common Greek consciousness' since the Bronze Age, and its 'pivotal role in the earliest Greek literature', see Pretzler, *Pausanias*, pp. 32-3.

[8] Xenophon, *Hellenika*, Book 5.1.32-3.

[9] Tozer, *Lectures*, p. 195.

the development of a considerable trade in such items as corn, wool, dried fish, slaves, and the timber essential for ship-building. Not all states were trading states, it is true; and it is noteworthy that Sparta was not among their number. But Athens, the greatest of the Greek states, was a trading state and was also notoriously dependent for much of its grain – not to mention timber and slaves – on supplies from the Black Sea region.[10] This led Athens to urge a common interest in the security from piracy of the trade routes and take the lead in policing them with its fleet when – for much of the fifth century – it was able to do so. And where trade was active and important, diplomacy readily took root. The mutually beneficial exchange of goods demonstrated the value of bargaining and fostered skill in the activity. It also required a minimum of settled regulation on the handling of disputes between traders and the property rights of a citizen in a foreign state, and demanded at least civil relations with those adjacent to trade routes such as the Hellespont.[11]

What kind of diplomacy was thrown up by these circumstances? The first and quite fundamental point to understand is that diplomacy was not regarded by the ancient Greeks as a distinctive and separate function of government; instead, it was seen simply as an aspect of general political activity. As a result, the city-states had nothing remotely resembling a ministry of foreign affairs or a diplomatic service. Not only in many states was policy fashioned in large councils and assemblies but it was also in such bodies that decisions on diplomatic appointments were made, instructions issued, and ambassadors quizzed on their return. Moreover, those sent abroad were given little public financial support and faced risks. Why, then, did they accept such burdens? The short answer is that, since most were principally politicians, they valued the civic prestige associated with diplomatic duties and also well understood the opportunities provided by them to further their own policies. It is to the personnel who carried out the diplomacy of ancient Greece – among whom the ambassadors were only one group – that we turn next.

Further reading

Adcock, Sir Frank and D. J. Mosley, *Diplomacy in Ancient Greece* (Thames and Hudson: London, 1975), Chs. 14 and 15

Anderson, J. K., *Xenophon* (Bristol Classical Press: London, 2001)

Berridge, G. R., *Diplomacy: Theory and Practice*, 6th ed (Palgrave Macmillan: Basingstoke, 2022), Introduction

Casson, Lionel, *Travel in the Ancient World* (Allen and Unwin: London, 1974)

Grant, J. R., 'A note on the tone of Greek diplomacy', *The Classical Quarterly*, New Series, 15 (2), November 1965

---

[10] According to Demosthenes, this made the Hellespont as vital to Athens as Thermopylae (the narrow coastal passage through which an invading army from the north had to pass), 'On the False Embassy', sec.180.

[11] The modern English name of which is the Dardanelles, in Turkish Çanakkale Boğazı.

Hamilton, K. and R. Langhorne, *The Practice of Diplomacy: Its evolution, theory and administration*, 2nd ed (Routledge: London and New York, 2011), Ch. 1

Hansen, M. H., *Polis: An introduction to the ancient Greek city-state* (Oxford University Press: Oxford, 2006)

Herodotus, *The Histories*, translated by Robin Waterfield with an Introduction and Notes by Carolyn Dewald (Oxford University Press: Oxford and New York, 1998)
An earlier English translation is available online.

Nicolson, Harold, *The Evolution of Diplomatic Method* (Constable: London, 1954), Ch. 1.

Ormerod, H. A., *Piracy in the Ancient World* (University of Liverpool Press: Liverpool; Hodder and Stoughton: London, 1924), pp. 96-150.

'Peloponnesian War', *Encyclopedia Britannica* [J. M. Mitchell] [www].

Phillipson, Coleman, *The International Law and Custom of Ancient Greece and Rome*, vol. I (Macmillan: London, 1911), Ch. 1 [www].

Powell, Anton, *Athens and Sparta: Constructing Greek political and social history from 478 BC*, 2nd ed (Routledge: London and New York, 2001)

Pretzler, Maria, *Pausanias: Travel writing in Ancient Greece* (Duckworth: London, 2007)

Rhodes, P. J., 'Political leagues (other than Sparta's)' in Xenophon's *Hellenika*, App. H in Xenophon: Strassler, R. B. (ed.), *The Landmark Xenophon's Hellenika*, trsl. by J. Marincola (Quercus: London, 2011)

Starr, Chester G., *The Influence of Sea Power on Ancient History* (Oxford University Press: New York and Oxford, 1989)

Toynbee, Arnold, *The Greeks and their Heritages* (Oxford University Press: Oxford, 1981), Ch. 4

Tozer, Rev. Henry Fanshawe, *Lectures on the Geography of Greece* (John Murray: London, 1873)

Watson, A., *Diplomacy: The dialogue between states* (Eyre Methuen: London, 1982), Ch. 7

Zimmern, Alfred, *The Greek Commonwealth: Politics and Economics in Fifth Century Athens*, 5th ed revised (Oxford University Press: Oxford, 1931)

1   Personnel

The diplomatic system of Ancient Greece employed three main kinds of representative: heralds, ambassadors or envoys, and *proxenoi*. The heralds were very different from the other two and, in light of their responsibility for preparing the way for ambassadors, it would seem natural to take them first. But the *proxenoi*, although attracting far less attention on the part of the ancient historians than the ambassadors, are not only the most interesting of Greek diplomatic agents but also quite possibly made a contribution to such stability as the Greek system enjoyed that was at least equal to that of the ambassadors. It is for these reasons that I begin this chapter with the institution of proxeny (*proxenia*).

Proxeny

Diplomatic *proxenoi* were chiefly the resident representatives of one city-state in another, although they were also appointed by other entities, including federations and merchants' associations. They probably first appeared in mainland Greece in the late seventh century, and their subsequent multiplication was in no small part connected with the great increase in international activity – especially commercial activity – before and especially after this juncture. By the middle of the fifth century the institution was firmly rooted in the whole Greek world and survived until its eclipse under the Roman occupation in the first century.

The numbers of *proxenoi* appointed are astonishing. Even very small states had widespread networks of them and, in states with which contact was very frequent, multiple appointments might be made. For example, at one point in the first half of the fourth century, Karthaia, a minor city on the Aegean island of Keos (today Kea), had more than 86 *proxenoi* scattered among other states, 15 of whom were found in Athens alone. During the Classical period, it is probable that all well-known Athenian politicians held one or more positions as *proxenos*. It has been estimated that over the 500 years or so that proxeny flourished, at least 1.2 million grants of *proxenia* in total were made in the Greek world.[12]

A city wishing to name a *proxenos* in another city invariably chose a man with a track record of being well-disposed towards it. This was usually a citizen of the other city whom its leaders might have befriended as a member of an embassy sent to them, as in the case of the Athenian, Cimon, who visited Sparta in this capacity as a young man in 479.[13] But sometimes a resident alien might be chosen – typically a wealthy merchant

---

[12]   Mack, *Proxeny and Polis*, pp. 14-15.
[13]   Kagan, *Pericles*, pp. 31-2.

The Greek States at the Outbreak of the Peloponnesian War, 431

such as Heracleides of Salamis, appointed as *proxenos* of Salamis by Athens in 325.[14] It can well be imagined how a state needing an active diplomacy in an emergency – as in Athens when its vital grain supply was threatened – would have cared little about the citizenship of a known benefactor willing to serve as a *proxenos*.

City-states appointed so many *proxenoi* in part because they served as a visible statement of their separate identities throughout the Greek world. The choice of a particular man as *proxenos* in a particular city – which choice was often contested by political factions in the nominating city – could also be a way of signalling a particular foreign policy. But these men provided many practical services as well, chief among them being assistance to visitors from the city to which they owed their position; these were private individuals, particularly merchants, as well as public officials, among them ambassadors. Their functions included confirming the identity of the visitors, providing them with advice and local information, opening doors to those with power and authority, and actually speaking on their behalf in law courts and before councils and

---

[14]   It should be added that, exceptionally, in Sparta it seems that a *proxenos* serving a foreign city was appointed not by that city but by the Spartan king himself.

assemblies in democracies and, where kings ruled, in the milieu of the royal court. In consequence, influential politicians and judges were particularly valued as *proxenoi*. In more disturbed times, they could be called on to assist with the ransom of captives. The *proxenos* was also bound to provide visitors from the city he served with food and shelter in his own house, which was doubly valuable because this surely 'served to strengthen the personal ties of the *proxenos* to leading members of the *polis* he represented'[15] – although hostelries of various kinds were increasingly available to foreigners in ancient Greece and such visitors were particularly welcome in Athens.

Box 1.1   Demosthenes, 384-322

Demosthenes was born into a rich Athenian family but his father died while he was very young and he was defrauded by his guardians of most of his inheritance. Having to earn a living from a trade, he became a professional speech writer for the law courts, and in 355 – although more adept at composing speeches than delivering them – commenced a glittering political career. Demosthenes believed that Athens should be an example to all Greece of civic virtue and democracy and that, because of its special talents, the city should lead the stand against tyranny from within as well as without the Hellenic world – but not impetuously, and via the law and diplomacy, with force as only a last resort. He regarded Philip of Macedon as the most serious external threat, and it was his anger at the deference shown to him by Aeschines that led him to charge his Athenian colleague with treason and cause such bitter and enduring rivalry between them. The Romans, who had read rather than listened to his speeches, 'admired him as a model, an instance of near-perfection in oratory' (Wardman, *Rome's Debt to Greece*, p. 112).

As the *proxenos* was the servant of a foreign state who roughly resembled the native dragoman of a European embassy in the much later Ottoman Empire, it should be no surprise that – like the dragoman – he always risked suspicion of disloyalty and sometimes courted danger in his own city. Thus was discomfited the great Athenian orator Demosthenes (Box 1.1) in 343, who was the *proxenos* in Athens for Thebes. At the second trial for treason of Aeschines (Box 1.2), engineered by Demosthenes, his rival had his revenge by describing Demosthenes as 'the paid servant of Thebes and the wickedest man in Hellas.'[16] Occasionally, a *proxenos* was murdered in his home city. Why, then, did prominent citizens accept – even actively seek – the appointment? In Athens they included Cimon, Alcibiades, and Callias as *proxenoi* for Sparta; Nicias for Syracuse; and Thraso as well as Demosthenes for Thebes. In Thessaly, Jason of Pherae, the coming strong man of Greece in the early fourth century, was *proxenos* of Sparta in Thessaly.

Box 1.2   Aeschines, 389-314

Aeschines was a native of Athens who rose through success both as a soldier and a clerkly servant of the city to be one of the most notable orators and statesmen of the age. He is remembered chiefly for his poisonous legal duels with Demosthenes, from which he eventually emerged the loser. This led to his voluntary exile on the Aegean island of Rhodes, later to that of Samos, where he died. An authoritative biographical sketch of Aeschines from the justly famous 1911 edition of the *Encyclopedia Britannica* can be found online.

---

[15]   Mack, *Proxeny and Polis*, p. 70.
[16]   Aeschines, 'On the Embassy', 2.143.

There were real advantages to receiving a grant of *proxenia*. Most valuable among these was that it highlighted foreign recognition of a citizen's importance and thereby added to his prestige at home. One consequence of this was that a *proxenos* could expect to be listened to with respect on policy towards the state, or states he represented. Eloquent evidence of the prestige attached to the position is the popularity of naming a child 'Proxenos'. But it also brought with it honours and privileges in the appointing city that were in some instances tantamount to the award of citizenship, if they did not – as often happened – provide full citizenship itself. By encouraging the *proxenos* to visit regularly and develop a stake in the appointing city, these were probably designed to nurture his warm feelings towards it. They typically included the right to own land, freedom from the taxes normally imposed on foreigners, unhindered access to decision-making bodies, a favoured seat at civic ceremonies, and – by no means least – the right of free and safe travel to the city he represented even should a state of war exist with his own. The *proxenos* might also receive valuable gifts of various sorts in gratitude for special services – and be granted asylum should the political situation at home turn ominously against him. As such a valuable asset to a family, it is not surprising that the position of *proxenos* was often passed down through generations of the same family. When Polydamus of Pharsalus arrived in Sparta to ask for military assistance, he began his address by reminding the Spartans that he was their *proxenos* and benefactor – like all his ancestors for as long as could be remembered. A similar opening remark on the same sort of occasion was made to the Spartans by Callias, their *proxenos* in Athens.

Such, then, were the advantages of the position that it was a risk well worth taking. In any case, severe hostility to a *proxenos* in his native city was comparatively rare. This was no doubt partly because so many members of each city-state's political elite were *proxenoi* that countenancing an attack on one would set a precedent that in due course might threaten any number of them. Another reason was that their role was acknowledged to amount to that of a near-genuine *intermediary* between their own state and the one of which they were *proxenos*; and this could become particularly important in war. Unambiguous evidence of this is the routine grant to the *proxenos*, already mentioned, of free and safe travel in peace *and in war*, whereby the appointing state exonerates in advance its *proxenos* from all personal blame for any harm caused to it by his fatherland. And, indeed, there is ample evidence of a *proxenos* being sent by his native city – whether in peace or war (or the more usual Greek position of something in between) – on diplomatic missions to the one he represented. For example, in 451 it was Cimon who negotiated Athens' badly needed Five Years' Peace with Sparta;[17] while Callias, a later Athenian *proxenos* of Sparta in his city, was sent at least three times

---

[17]   Kagan, *Pericles*, pp. 92-3.

as ambassador to Sparta;[18] as, it seems likely, was Polydamus of Pharsalus.[19] Further instances are found in the account of the Peloponnesian War by the great historian, Thucydides. Nymphodorus, the *proxenos* for Athens in Thrace during the war, had great influence with its king, Sitalces; he visited Athens and played a key role in bringing over to the Athenians not only this ruler but also the king of Macedonia; while Lichias, *proxenos* of the Argives in Sparta, was sent by the Spartans to Argos with proposals either for war or peace.[20]

But was the *proxenos* a 'true intermediary'? Mack frequently refers to him as 'an intermediary' by way of summing up the numerous services he provided.[21] But when using the term 'true intermediary' after stressing the customary right of safe passage in peace or war provided by appointing states, he is careful to say that it was thus that he was 'cast' in this role.[22] In other words, the appointing state wished the *proxenos* to regard himself in this light – as a man who owed *equal loyalty to both states*. This seems right because this was clearly in the interests of the appointing state. Equally clearly, in most cases it was probably only wishful thinking. Having said that, if anyone came close to being a genuine intermediary in a bilateral relationship – as opposed to an impartial third party introduced into it – it was the *proxenos*.

Was the *proxenos* unique, or was he the prototype – as is commonly suggested – of the modern honorary consul? The case for the latter, which is strong, is that, like the *proxenos*, the honorary consul is usually a citizen of the state where he is appointed to operate (with an equal possibility of having 'dual nationality'), likewise unsalaried, and similarly expected to give much time to assisting visitors, some of whom might have become permanent residents. However, unlike the *proxenos*, who was the only resident representative of a foreign state extant at the time, few if any honorary consuls have heavy, high-level political responsibilities as well. It is the latter that begin to drag the ancient Greek institution more towards resembling the modern ambassador, and thereby makes the *proxenos* a distinctive type of diplomatic agent: honorary consul, ambassador and lobbyist all rolled into one.

Heralds

As for the heralds (*kerykes*), they were regarded as the offspring of Hermes, the messenger of the gods, and carried a staff (*caduceus*) as the symbol of their office.[23] They

---

18   Xenophon, *Hellenika*, Book 6.3.4; Phillipson, *International Law and Custom*, pp. 153-4.
19   Xenophon, *Hellenika*, Book 6.1.4.
20   Thucydides, *Peloponnesian War*, pp. 113-14 [2.29.1], 354 [5.76.3]. Other examples, particularly of *proxenoi* employed in peace negotiations, are provided by Mack, *Proxeny and Polis*, p. 117, n. 109.
21   Mack, *Proxeny and Polis*, p. 48, for example.
22   Mack, *Proxeny and Polis*, p. 128.
23   'Caduceus', *Encyclopedia Britannica*.

were general-purpose messengers and masters of ceremonies, and so needed a powerful voice; among other things, they made announcements at Panhellenic games. And not all of the tasks that took them abroad were of a diplomatic nature; they might, for example, have to serve as a propagandist or transmitter of orders to soldiers on a battlefront. They are not to be confused with messengers pure and simple (*angeloi*), who were probably any trusted and fit citizens who could be enlisted as and when the need arose.[24]

The diplomatic responsibilities of the heralds were heavy and one of these was to serve as a 'truce-bearer' prior to the start of the Panhellenic games (see Chapter 3). More important still was their task of going ahead of ambassadors in order to secure guarantees for their safe reception. Usually working alone, they were able to undertake this dangerous work because they were believed to enjoy divine protection and probably because this and their other duties were more technical than political. Heralds also represented an institution which self-evidently served all cities equally. Nevertheless, they were more at risk when relations were particularly tense and it was sometimes judged prudent to stipulate in an armistice that their safe conduct should be guaranteed. It has been said that the unusual degree of immunity which they enjoyed applied even to those from non-Greek states such as Persia.[25] They often came from important families which had held the office through generations but despite this, and despite their sanctity, heralds did not *have* to be received, although they usually were. Thucydides says that

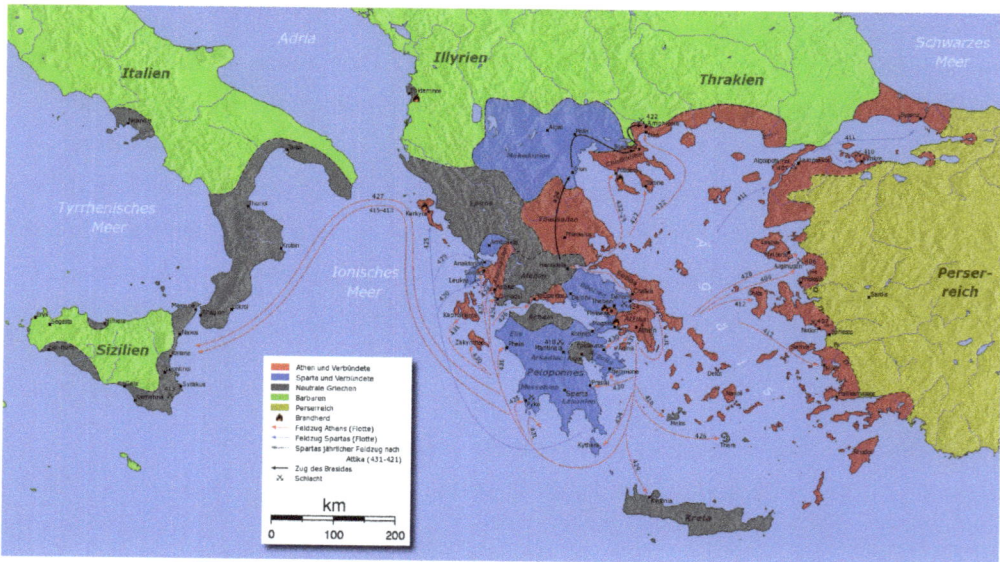

The Peloponnesian War

---

[24] 'Barbarian' ambassadors were usually described as mere *angeloi*, Adcock and Mosley, *Diplomacy in Ancient Greece*, p. 152. This is presumably for the same reason that non-Greeks were described as 'barbarians'.

[25] Frey and Frey, *The History of Diplomatic Immunity*, p. 16.

once the Peloponnesian War started there was 'no further communication between the two sides except through heralds.'[26] Although this strong statement is contradicted at numerous points by his own history, it seems clear that heralds were certainly the chief mode of communication between the Athenians and the Spartans and their respective allies. In this as in other conflicts, they were responsible not only for issuing ultimatums and declarations of war, and seeking permission for the removal of the dead from a battlefield; but also for conducting dialogues – for example, on the proper treatment of consecrated ground following fighting. When their tasks followed a well-understood formula they were probably allowed to rely on memory to convey their messages but when these were more complicated or there was a fear that poor command of language or an inability to resist the temptation to say what they believed would be popular, it is possible that they carried letters.[27]

Ambassadors

When the need arose and heralds had – where necessary – secured guarantees for their safety, ambassadors were appointed; although if the need was urgent and there was reasonable confidence in their reception, ambassadors already designated might be hot on a herald's heels.[28] In Athens, ambassadors were elected rather than chosen by lot. They were also given credentials to certify their status.

As elsewhere until the late fifteenth century AD, ambassadors were not sent abroad to establish permanent missions and deal with general business, including general information-gathering. Instead, their responsibility was solely to discharge specific tasks, whereupon – unless deliberately detained by their hosts to prevent them carrying away damaging intelligence[29] – they usually departed promptly for home. It is true that a city of special importance might be visited so often as to make it easy to jump to the conclusion that the envoys had virtually created a resident mission. Such, for example, might be supposed to have been the consequence of the frequent visits of Athenian ambassadors to the Persian city of Susa (modern day Shush near the head of the Persian Gulf) in the late fifth century.[30] But even were these visits to have been frequent and conducted by the same individuals, they could not have produced the

---

[26] Thucydides, *Peloponnesian War*, p. 97 [2.1.1.].

[27] These were certainly considerations which, according to Thucydides, disposed Nicias, one of the Athenian generals leading the fateful expedition to Sicily late in the fifth century, to send home 'messengers' with a letter, *Peloponnesian War*, pp. 437-8 [7.8.2]. These men would not have been heralds, but heralds would have presented the same risk.

[28] This, according to Demosthenes, was the case with the first official Athenian embassy to Macedonia, 'On the False Embassy', 19.163.

[29] Xenophon, *Hellenika*, 1.4.4-7.

[30] See Wilamowitz, *Reden und Vorträge*, p. 44, endorsed by both Zimmern, *The Greek Commonwealth*, p. 372, n. 1; Bozeman, *Politics and Culture in International History*, p. 77; and Badian, 'The Peace of Callias', p. 14.

local knowledge, contacts, and opportunities for unobtrusive engagement available to a genuine resident mission. At best this was a half-way house towards modern diplomacy. The ambassadors of ancient Greece were what today we would call special envoys, envoys limited in time and function.

Sometimes with full powers to conclude without reference home, the chief task of an ancient Greek embassy was typically one (or sometimes more) of the following: securing a new ruler's friendship on his accession to office; negotiating a treaty, perhaps for an alliance or a peace settlement; giving or receiving oaths for a treaty already concluded; soliciting agreement to act as an arbitrator; or stiffening the resolve of an imperilled ally or calling on another for urgent help or an explanation of a change of course. The ambassadors of powerful cities were also not above directly interfering in the domestic affairs of another. A case in point is the order to stop work given to the men rebuilding the city walls of Athens by an embassy from Sparta. This was prompted by Sparta's fear of the great rise in the military prestige of Athens that followed the defeat of the Persians by the Hellenes in 480 and the failure of the Spartan embassy to secure the agreement of the Athenian *boule* (council of 500) to issue the order itself.

Greek envoys were usually senior and respected members of the assemblies or more limited membership councils in which foreign policy was shaped; the first term to describe them was the word for elders, *presbeis*. Such was the value attached to the experience and wisdom needed by an envoy that in some states the office had a high minimum age; in Chalcidice, for example, ambassadors had to be at least 50 years old. Some men appointed as ambassadors already held important offices in the state, typically that of general (*strategos*) when it was thought essential to impress a powerful state such as the Persian Empire. Those who had a special interest in foreign policy, such as Callias and Demosthenes in Athens and Antalcidas ('a specialist in Persian diplomacy'[31]) in Sparta, tended to be sent on embassies repeatedly; others might serve on just one or two. However, if a mission did not involve discussion of high policy and was only concerned with a matter such as the reception of oaths, it seems to have been customary to appoint more junior figures.

Perhaps the most significant features of these embassies were the large size and varied composition of their 'diplomatic staff'.[32] Spartan embassies generally employed only three ambassadors but this was unusual. Those of other cities, among them Athens, could despatch embassies with as many as ten or eleven members, the latter number – as in the case of the first official Athenian embassy to Philip of Macedon in 346 – not being rare; this was especially so when great importance attached to the mission and flattery was a consideration. Furthermore, such large embassies characteristically represented

[31] Xenophon, *Hellenika*, App. M, p. 398.
[32] Their suites were also probably large, Phillipson, *International Law and Custom*, pp. 327-8.

different points of view on policy towards the state for which they were destined.[33] They could also include a representative of an allied state, as one from Tenedos – allied to Athens in the faltering Second Athenian League – was chosen to represent all of the allies on the embassies to Macedon.[34] These embassies were a bilateral variant of the species of multilateral diplomacy that in the early twenty-first century AD it became fashionable to call 'multi-stakeholder diplomacy'. Harold Nicolson called them 'mixed embassies' and deplored the possibility they gave their host of playing off one faction in a mission against another. 'It seems curious to us,' he wrote, 'that intelligent people should have permitted so bad a diplomatic method to survive.'[35]

As it happens, the Greeks were not always so stupid as to send an embassy abroad without giving thought – even if sometimes belated – to the impact of its composition on the outcome sought. For example, in 336 the Athenians sent an embassy to placate Alexander, who had succeeded as ruler of Macedon following the assassination of his father, Philip. Demosthenes, who was well known for his hostility to Macedon, set off as a member of this mission but turned back before it arrived at Alexander's camp. This may have been because of fear, as Aeschines charged, but 'his absence made it easier for Alexander to give the envoys a favorable reply.'[36] Nevertheless, the mixed character of most embassies could indeed be exploited by their hosts. Did it have compensating advantages?

It should be noted to begin with that these Greek embassies were not usually as anarchic as Nicolson implies. For one thing, it was normal for them to have a leader, often the man whose proposal for the embassy led to its appointment. For example:

- Hegesippus, a violent opponent of Macedon, was the acknowledged leader of an Athenian embassy sent in 343 to Pella, the seat of Philip II, to demand re-negotiation of a peace settlement of three years earlier (the Peace of Philocrates) which had also allied Athens to his kingdom[37]
- Demosthenes, then at the height of his influence, was on his own motion sent as 'leader of an embassy to seek an alliance with the Thebans' following the alarming news reaching Athens in late 339 that Philip had taken the Phocian town of Elatea, and

---

[33] The members of the first official Athenian embassy to Macedon are detailed in Buckler, 'Demosthenes and Aeschines', pp. 119-20, while something of its internal dynamics is revealed in Aeschines, 'On the Embassy'.

[34] Aeschines, 'On the Embassy', 2.20.

[35] Nicolson, *Evolution of Diplomatic Method*, pp. 6-7.

[36] Sealey, *Demosthenes*, p. 202. Aeschines says that he 'came running home – useless in peace and war alike!', 'Against Ctesiphon', 3.161.

[37] Demosthenes, 'On the False Embassy', 19.331.

- Demades, similarly appointed on his own motion, in 335 'headed' an Athenian embassy to the Macedonians.[38]

In books 11 to 14 alone of the history of Diodorus the Sicilian, there is mention of five embassies led by one envoy or another. It is true that this is but a fraction of the embassies that flit across his pages like gnats on a summer evening but he reports them in such a matter of fact way as to suggest that this was the norm.[39]

Should a mission prove successful, embassy leadership was commonly signified by attaching the name of the leader to the treaty that issued from it, especially if it were a peace treaty. Notable examples include the Peace of Callias between Athens and Persia (449),[40] the Peace of Nicias between Athens and Sparta (421) (Box 1.3), the Peace of Antalcidas between Sparta and Persia (387),[41] and the Peace of Philocrates between Athens and Macedon (346).[42]

Box 1.3 Nicias, c. 470-414/13

Nicias, an immensely wealthy man, became leader of the aristocratic party in Athens after the death in 429 of the formidable Pericles, with whom he had worked closely and whose style he took great trouble to imitate. He also served as a general during the Peloponnesian War. He was cautious, shrewd, incorruptible, deeply religious, public-spirited and no coward – but he was neither engaging nor charismatic. His qualities served him better as a framer of foreign policy and diplomat than as a soldier, although he had some successes even in the latter role. He was *proxenos* for the foremost city-state on the island of Sicily, the Greek city of Syracuse; and an important if eventually unsuccessful check on the imperialist dreamers at Athens. In 421 he played a prominent role in successfully negotiating a one-year truce in the Peloponnesian War with the much-weakened Spartans, and then a peace settlement that bore his name – the Peace of Nicias. When certain important cities refused to enter this agreement, it was expanded into an alliance with the Spartans and, when the war party in Athens revived, Nicias led an embassy to Sparta in an attempt to obtain sufficient concessions to undermine its support; however, in this he failed. It is one of the many ironies of history that the last great adventure of the *proxenos* for Syracuse was his joint command of a major Athenian expedition to Sicily in 415. The major – if unstated – aim of this was to seize Syracuse and thereby control of the whole of that large island. It was also a command that fell to him alone during a period following the loss of his two fellow generals and before he was joined by another. Nicias had, in fact, strongly opposed the whole idea, preferring – as a true conservative – that Athens should enjoy what it had rather than expose itself to a Spartan attack by dividing its forces in the interests of a far-flung enterprise on which the omens were not good. If the Athenian fleet had to be sent at all, he believed, it should simply cruise around the island, and – having put its peoples in awe by what sea powers millennia later would call a 'naval demonstration' – return home. Thucydides reports that this strategy was still much in his mind during the operation, but demoralized his men. In the event, Nicias failed to take decisive action, a Spartan general intervened, and the expedition was a disaster. Nicias was captured and – although some voices urged clemency towards him on the grounds of his previous service to Syracuse, support for peace with Sparta, and opposition to the expedition – he was put to death.

---

[38] Sealey, *Demosthenes*, pp. 196, 203.

[39] Diodorus Siculus: *The Persian Wars*, pp. 47, 96, 134-5, 210, 293. Two others are named in footnotes by Peter Green, the historian and translator of this edition: pp. 154, 273.

[40] Assuming this was not a fiction, Powell, *Athens and Sparta*, pp. 49-53.

[41] Also known as 'the King's Peace'.

[42] Philocrates had conducted a lengthy campaign in the assembly for negotiations with Philip of Macedon, which eventually led to the despatch of the first official Athenian embassy to Pella in 346. The second embassy, sent to receive Philip's oaths to the treaty, was composed of the same men, Buckler, 'Demosthenes and Aeschines', pp. 117, 119-20, 134; Ryder, 'Demosthenes and Philip II', pp. 58-6.

It is also likely that some members of an embassy would have had greater age and experience than their fellows (Demosthenes and Aeschines were the youngest members of the first embassy to Philip of Macedon), so they would have carried more weight even if they held no formal leadership position. Unless for some special reason it was agreed otherwise, naturally these elders spoke first in formal encounters with representatives of the city to which they were sent. With a leader, even a mixed embassy would have found it somewhat easier to preserve a show of unity abroad. And a leader had another interest in pressing the embassy's factions to fall into line: his anxiety to have them share the responsibility for its actions when the embassy returned home. This is evident from the attitude of Demosthenes following both the first and second official Athenian embassies to Macedonia.[43]

With or without a leader, the typically mixed character of the Greek embassy was a blessing as well as a curse. Being so obviously representative of the people from whom it had come, it was likely to command respect, especially in a city which also had a democratic constitution. Furthermore, it was more likely to reassure the host government that any agreement made with it would be ratified without serious difficulty – and also ratified by the assemblies of any allies represented on the embassy. A special case of the mixed embassy was the joint embassy of two states needing arbitration of a dispute sent to a third state they hoped to persuade to accept the responsibility.[44] None of the ancient historians and no latter day scholar other than Harold Nicolson seems to have thought the 'mixed' character of the Greek embassies to have been a serious diplomatic handicap.

The unexceptional, essentially political nature of the work of these Greek embassies is further suggested by the fact that, compared to the embassies of Rome and Byzantium, no elaborate protocol marked the occasion of their despatch. Nor could they expect special treatment on their passage through third states or in their reception at their destinations.

There was no general rule that ambassadors were safe from official molestation in passing through the territory of third parties on their journeys. Indeed, ambassadors themselves could encourage the arrest of ambassadors of an enemy state or alliance, as in the case of the Peloponnesian ambassadors en route to Persia in 430 who were detained in Thrace at the request of two Athenian ambassadors, then taken to Athens where they were all executed.[45] In 397, the Spartans had their revenge, intercepting an embassy en

---

43 Adcock and Mosley, *Diplomacy in Ancient Greece*, pp. 159-60; Sealey, *Demosthenes*, pp. 11-12; Ryder, 'Demosthenes and Philip II', pp. 61-70; Aeschines, 'Against Ctesiphon', 3.63. It is true, however, if Aeschines is to be believed, that at a private meeting of the Athenian ambassadors prior to appearing before Philip (on their second mission) it was agreed that each should speak his own mind to the Macedonian king. He also reported Demosthenes as declaring in his own speech before Philip that the members of the embassy were not all of one mind, 'On the Embassy', 2.107, 2.109.

44 Tod, *International Arbitration*, p. 83.

45 Thucydides, *Peloponnesian War*, p. 136 [2.67.1-4].

route to Persia sponsored by the war party in Athens and executing its members.[46] If a journey was likely to be dangerous, special permission needed to be obtained and on the sea this appears to have been impractical. Ambassadors would generally set off with only the reassurance that – provided their visit was heralded – their hosts would be required to protect them under the traditional code of hospitality demanded by Zeus, even should they come from an unfriendly city. But this assumed that they behaved themselves as guests: they had no freedom from arrest and punishment for breaking local laws, and thus no diplomatic immunity in the modern sense.

Elaborate protocol no more surrounded the reception than the despatch of ambassadors. Other than a possible dinner or seat at an entertainment, the rules of hospitality did not extend to the provision of food and shelter; for these they generally had to rely on their own resources or those of their *proxenos*. Because of the fear of the use to which the charge of accepting bribes could be put by their political enemies at home, there was also a taboo on the acceptance by ambassadors of gifts – at any rate lavish ones – from their hosts.

In the absence of a foreign ministry and because of the usual paucity of reliable information on foreign states from other sources (see Box 1.4), Greek ambassadors bore heavy responsibilities towards their own cities. Demosthenes said that an envoy was not only responsible for faithfully following his instructions from the assembly and acting in a timely manner because opportunities for pressing an advantage were often fleeting; on his return, he was also responsible for providing an accurate report on his mission and trustworthy advice on policy to be followed in light of its results.[47] Ambassadors sometimes had to return home or send back messengers if they felt the need for new instructions, although at least in the case of Athens they were allowed some discretion in adjusting their negotiations to cope with unforeseen circumstances.[48]

Box 1.4   Corinth: centre of trade – and foreign intelligence
A significant exception to this general rule was the wealthy city of Corinth, which lay close to the narrowest section of the neck of land (isthmus) separating the Peloponnese from the northern part of mainland Greece. In about 600, a stone causeway (*diolkos*) was built across this, thus enabling goods and even ships on the east-west route to be hauled from the Gulf of Corinth to the Saronic Gulf instead of having to take the long and dangerous journey around the southern tip of the Peloponnese. In consequence a great centre of transit trade as well as of trade on its own account, Corinth obtained 'excellent access to information and to the ears of leading figures from other states' (Kagan, *Pericles*, p. 76). By the time of the outbreak of the Peloponnesian War in 431, Corinth was also second only to Athens as a Greek naval power.

---

[46]   Bruce, 'Athenian embassies', pp. 272, 276-7.
[47]   Demosthenes alleged that Aeschines, having been bribed by Philip, had fallen down on all four counts, 'On the False Embassy', 19.8.
[48]   Aeschines says of the first official Athenian embassy to Macedonia that its 'decree' contained the following instruction: 'The ambassadors shall also negotiate concerning any good thing that may be within their power', 'On the Embassy', 2.104.

In Athens, ambassadors – like military commanders – were responsible to the law courts and could be charged with criminal behaviour. This might not only be that they had acted treasonously, accepted lavish bribes or pretended to hold their office after it had terminated but also that they had exceeded their instructions, concluded a treaty on unfavourable terms, or even agreed to one that seemed satisfactory at the time but later turned out badly. Such risks probably had more serious consequences for the diplomacy of Athens – and other city-states where similar conditions obtained – than 'mixed embassies'. It probably discouraged some able men from accepting nomination in the first place, sometimes inhibited the negotiations of those who did undertake them, and led to the loss of men unfairly condemned for the manner in which they had conducted a mission. Some were fined, some banished, and some even executed. Philocrates, following the reappraisal by the Athenian assembly of the treaty with Philip of Macedon in 346 which bore his name, fled into exile to avoid facing trial and was condemned to death in his absence.[49] Perhaps only because Aeschines was a brilliant orator was he able to secure his own acquittal in the face of Demosthenes's charges. Nicolson was certainly right to observe that it was 'no sinecure to serve as the ambassador of a Greek City State.'[50]

Further reading

Proxeny

Adcock, Sir Frank and D. J. Mosley, *Diplomacy in Ancient Greece* (Thames and Hudson: London, 1975), pp. 160-3

Gardner, P. and F. B. Jevons, *A Manual of Greek Antiquities* (Scribner's: New York, 1895), pp. 597-9 [www].

Kagan, Donald, *Pericles of Athens and the Birth of Democracy* (Secker and Warburg: London, 1990), pp. 31-47 *passim*, on Cimon as proxenos of Sparta in Athens

Kralli, Ionna, 'Athenian proxeny decrees'. Review of E. Culasso Gastaldi, *Le prossenie ateniesi del IV secolo a.C. Gli onorati asiatici* (2004), *The Classical Review*, 56 (2), October, 2006

Mack, William, *Proxeny and Polis: Institutional Networks in the Ancient Greek World* (Oxford University Press: Oxford, 2015)

Phillipson, Coleman, *The International Law and Custom of Ancient Greece and Rome*, vol. I (Macmillan: London, 1911), pp. 147-56 [www].

Plutarch's Lives, vol. 3 ('Cimon')

Proxeny Networks of the Ancient World (a database of proxeny networks of the Greek city-states) [www].

Wallace, M. B., 'Early Greek *proxenoi*', *Phoenix*, vol. 24, 1970

Xenophon: Strassler, R. B. (ed.), *The Landmark Xenophon's Hellenika*, trsl. by J. Marincola (Quercus: London, 2011), index refs. '*proxenos*'. A much earlier translation, published in 1891 by H.G. Daykins, is available in Wikisource [www], but there is no index.

---

[49] Earlier in the fourth century (392/1) the peace-minded Athenian envoy to Sparta, Andocides, together with his colleagues, was forced to adopt the same expedient, Adcock and Mosley, *Diplomacy in Ancient Greece*, p. 69.

[50] *Evolution of Diplomatic Method*, p. 6.

Heralds

Adcock, Sir Frank and D. J. Mosley, *Diplomacy in Ancient Greece* (Thames and Hudson: London, 1975), pp. 152-3, 201-2

'Caduceus', *Encyclopedia Britannica, 1911 edition* [www].

Frey, Linda S. and Marsha L. Frey, *The History of Diplomatic Immunity* (Ohio State University Press: Columbus, 1999), Intro. and Ch. 1

Remijsen, Sofie and Willy Clarysse, 'Heralds and trumpeters', *Ancient Olympics* [www].

Ambassadors

Adcock, Sir Frank and D. J. Mosley, *Diplomacy in Ancient Greece* (Thames and Hudson: London, 1975), pp. 152-62, 214-16

Aeschines, 'On the Embassy' [www].

Badian, E., 'The Peace of Callias', *The Journal of Hellenic Studies*, vol. 107, 1987

Bruce, I. A. F., 'Athenian embassies in the early fourth century B.C.', *Historia*, 15 (3), August 1966

Buckler, John, 'Demosthenes and Aeschines', in Worthington, I. (ed), *Demosthenes: Statesman and orator* (Routledge: London and New York, 2000)

'Demosthenes', *Encyclopedia Britannica* [R. C. Jebb] [www].

Demosthenes, 'On the False Embassy' [www].

Frey, Linda S. and Marsha L. Frey, *The History of Diplomatic Immunity* (Ohio State University Press: Columbus, 1999), pp. 18-19

Nicolson, Harold, *The Evolution of Diplomatic Method* (Constable: London, 1954), Ch. 1

Phillipson, Coleman, *The International Law and Custom of Ancient Greece and Rome*, vol. I (Macmillan: London, 1911), Ch. 13 [www].

Rung, Edward, 'The Mission of Philiscus to Greece in 369/8 B.C.', *Anabasis. Studia classica et orientalia*, vol. 4, 2014 [www].

Rung, Edward, 'War, peace and diplomacy in Graeco-Persian relations from the sixth to the fourth century BC', in Philp de Souza and John France (eds), *War and Peace in the Ancient World* (Cambridge University Press: Cambridge, 2008)

Ryder, T. T. B., 'Demosthenes and Philip II', in Worthington, I. (ed), *Demosthenes: Statesman and orator* (Routledge: London and New York, 2000)

Sealey, R., *Demosthenes: A study in defeat* (Oxford University Press: New York, 1993)

2 Bilaterals – private as well as public

How did the ambassadors described in the previous chapter go about pressing their cases on the ruling bodies of other city-states? What, in other words, was the characteristic style of the bilateral diplomacy of the ancient Greeks?

The common assumption is that the typical embassy of ancient Greece sought agreement to its demands by means of set speeches before popular assemblies that were delivered by each of its members in turn and crafted by schooling in the new art of rhetoric. This accomplished, they retired during the subsequent debate and returned only when it was completed. 'During the period of Greek liberty,' says Nicolson, 'diplomatic negotiations were conducted orally and, at least in theory, with full publicity.'[51] Is it true, therefore, that their task was merely UN General Assembly-style 'open' or 'parliamentary' diplomacy, or was there, as Nicolson hints, a significant degree of private negotiation as well? But, whether this is true or not, its public face was certainly the most distinctive feature of the diplomacy of the ancient Greeks and so must be considered first.

Open diplomacy and the art of rhetoric

Undoubtedly the great formal authority and real weight of citizen assemblies in decision-making in most Greek city-states in the classical period obliged embassies to address them openly, and therefore to take particular trouble over their oratory. Public oratory might even be required in city-states, Macedon for one, that were not democracies and so had no popular assembly. Thus Aeschines reports that when the individual members of the second official Athenian embassy to Macedonia addressed Philip they did so in the presence of ambassadors from other cities, among them Thebes, the current military operations of which were at the top of the embassy's agenda. 'All Hellas is watching to see what will happen,' he claims to have privately warned his fellow envoys.[52] The quality of oratory was also of great importance to the advocates of the contestant states making their cases to the arbitral tribunals of third states that were so numerous in ancient Greece (see Chapter 3), the more so because time limits were placed on their speeches.[53] More and more, therefore, attention had to be given to *rhetoric*, which, it should be added, was as vital to political success at home as it was to diplomatic success abroad.

---

51   Nicolson, *Evolution of Diplomatic Method*, p. 7.
52   Aeschines, 'On the Embassy', 2.104 (see also 2.112).
53   Tod, *International Arbitration*, pp. 122-3.

Rhetoric was the name given to the art of winning over a jury or popular assembly by the employment of a variety of techniques beyond reliance on evidence and logic; in short, the art of winning even with a weak case. The techniques of persuasion included the choice of resonant metaphors, verbal tricks such as appealing to general probability ('Is it really likely that a weak city such as ours would have deliberately broken our treaty with you?'), a tone of delivery (perhaps angry) that appealed to the emotions, and a peroration so crafted as to leave the orator's argument firmly lodged even in the heads of those listeners who had failed to grasp its more subtle components.[54] Sensitivity to rhetoric appeared in the middle of the fifth century and gave birth to a class of professional speech-writers and teachers of rhetoric ('rhetoricians'), among which the Sophists were prominent. The art of rhetoric reached its highest expression in the thought of Aristotle in the middle of the fourth century, although – unlike many rhetoricians – the great philosopher still favoured emphasis on the persuasive power of the truth.

For certain tasks, such as securing agreement in principle to an alliance or calling for help under the terms of an existing treaty, an ambassadorial speech shaped and coloured even by modest gestures to the new art of rhetoric might have been all, or just about all, that was needed. For example, when Sparta sent an envoy to Athens with an urgent plea for assistance against Thebes under a treaty of 371, the assembly 'was swayed by the appeal and voted to send Iphikrates with a force.'[55] It might well be, however, that the significance of public negotiation in ancient Greece has been exaggerated, probably because the texts of public orations – real or inferred – have survived much more readily than any records of private negotiations and are famously prominent in the history of the Peloponnesian War compiled by the Athenian general, Thucydides, on whom so much reliance is inevitably placed.[56]

Private negotiations

In his biography of legendary Pericles, the dominant figure in Athenian politics in the middle years of the fifth century, Donald Kagan remarks matter-of-factly that as 'a diplomat, he negotiated public treaties and secret agreements …'.[57] And the small states seem to have been particularly fearful of the 'secret diplomacy' of their greater brethren.[58]

---

[54] A sadly effective modern example, which whipped his 2016 campaign trail audiences into a mindless frenzy, is Donald Trump's 'Let's make America great again' slogan.
[55] Sealey, *Demosthenes*, p. 71.
[56] On the reasons for this, see Westlake, 'Diplomacy in Thucydides', pp. 227-35.
[57] Kagan, *Pericles*, p. 6.
[58] Aeschines, 'On the Embassy', 2.120.

There is evidence that some important embassies – even those sent from one democracy to another – were never invited to address a public assembly at all. More importantly, there is also evidence that, even when they were so invited, a great deal of private negotiation also took place between ambassadors and much smaller groups of office holders and influential individuals.[59] This was preliminary to or designed to follow up public debate – or both. In Athens itself the council of five hundred (or its presiding committee) was the first port of call of visiting envoys and it was here that they were interrogated as to the object of their mission and a decision made as to whether they should be permitted to address the assembly; many matters were actually left to the discretion of the council. It is true that set speeches were made before the council as well but it could and sometimes did meet in secret session. At oligarchical Sparta, there was also a citizen assembly but it was much less powerful, and probably even more decisive in private dealings with foreign ambassadors was the role played by the five ephors, the annually elected senior officers who, together with its two kings, ruled the state; here, personal foreign friendships could be important (see Box 2.1).

Box 2.1   Personal friendship and private negotiations
Where democracy was at a discount, as in Sparta and Persia, and personal ties with powerful foreigners were close, it seems doubly safe to assume that private negotiations between them were of great importance. A famous case in point is the friendship between the Spartan admiral, Lysander, and the Persian satrap, Cyrus, who had learned to speak Greek. This played an important role in Persia's decision to throw its weight against Athens in the final stage of the Peloponnesian War. It is also interesting to muse on what bearing – if any – the well-known personal friendship between Pericles and King Archidamus II of Sparta had on the private negotiations between their two states that preceded and sought to prevent this war. Within Greece there were many opportunities for personal friendships to be struck up between leading citizens of different states, among them shared commands in allied military operations (especially against 'barbarians'), Panhellenic public festivals (see Ch. 3), and encounters on embassies. 'Guest-friendships' (*xenia*) thus established were passed on through the generations.

Even in quiet periods, complex questions such as the naval and financial contributions to leagues would probably have been less amenable to settlement by public oratory. But in war and other unsettled times decision-making on all questions – including proposals from foreign ambassadors – could for long periods by-pass altogether not only an assembly but also a council, and devolve to individuals and small, secretive groups.[60] Since officials controlled access to the assembly, it is also a reasonable supposition that when an embassy about which there was special anxiety was allowed to address the people this was because – unless they had simply been forced to permit it by pressure from allied cities – certain understandings about what would be said had

---

[59]   This is the burden of Westlake's valuable 'Diplomacy in Thucydides'.
[60]   Adcock and Mosley, *Diplomacy in Ancient Greece*, p. 171.

already been agreed; in Athens even in normal times the council had the right to frame a resolution to guide discussion of an embassy's business. There was any number of reasons for the increase in secret negotiations at the expense of the popular assembly in wartime and Thucydides provides us with numerous examples from the Peloponnesian War.

For one thing, secret negotiations made it possible to secure a new ally without prematurely arousing the ire of an old one, as in the case of the dealings with embassies from Boeotia and Corinth of certain Spartan ephors opposed to the peace with Athens and of those on a later occasion of Chios with Sparta, also at the expense of Athens.[61] Secret discussions also made it easier to prevent the sabotage of a policy which was expected to be unpopular at home. Thus, to the disgust of the Athenian envoys, their wartime negotiations on Melos were conducted privately because it suited the Melian 'governing body and the few' to conceal from their people that they intended to take the huge risk – which in the event proved fatal – of refusing absorption into the Athenian empire.[62] For similar reasons, while a privately negotiated understanding between a visiting embassy and an influential individual might not pre-empt an assembly presentation, it could 'fix' the debate and thus have the same effect. Such was the result of the private negotiations between the powerful Athenian, Alcibiades, and the Spartan embassy which visited Athens in the twelfth year of the war.[63] Another advantage of secret negotiations was saving face with allies, which was of great concern to the Spartans following the Athenian victory over them at Pylos. They were granted an armistice and allowed to send ambassadors to Athens to sue for a general peace. However, they asked to negotiate its separate points with a committee rather than with the assembly because they were not optimistic of success and did not wish their proposed concessions to get them 'a bad name' with their allies to no purpose. The procedure was refused by the Athenians and the Spartans departed – but, according to Thucydides, Athens was later to regret this decision. Secret negotiations could also spare the public humiliation of a rejected suitor and avoid its possibly dangerous consequences. This was presumably why, following the first peace and alliance between the Athenians and the Spartans, the democratic Argives adopted the discreet suggestion of the Corinthians that, rather than employ their popular assembly for the purpose, they should use 'a few people with special powers' to negotiate the entry of any suitably qualified Hellenic state into a defensive alliance with them. All Thucydides tells us is that the reason for this was to preserve secrecy 'in the cases of those whose applications

---

61   Thucydides, *Peloponnesian War*, pp. 330 [5.36.1], 493 [8.7.1].
62   Thucydides, *Peloponnesian War*, p. 359 [5.8.43].
63   Thucydides, *Peloponnesian War*, p. 336 [5.45.1-4].

for alliance were not accepted' – but the meaning seems clear enough.[64] In the following century, Alcibiades and Demosthenes were both active in this kind of private diplomacy.[65]

Before leaving the topic of private negotiation in ancient Greece it is also interesting to note the numerous occasions on which embassies regularly bumped into each other on missions to the same city – especially Athens, Sparta, Argos and Thebes – thereby providing a further opportunity for secret bilateral diplomacy. This might have been because they had different business in the same city at the same time; because they had been summoned for a particular purpose by one of the leading states;[66] or – admittedly less likely – because a counter-embassy was hurriedly despatched to a third state when it was learned that ambassadors from a rival were heading for it.[67] As to the significance of these circumstances, it seems sufficient to record the observation of Thucydides that there were many discussions between the numerous embassies present in Sparta at the juncture in the eleventh year of the Peloponnesian War when the Lacedaemonians were having second thoughts about the alliance they had made with Athens in 421, the Peace of Nicias.[68] The historian obviously saw nothing remarkable in this sort of private discussion between embassies happening to find themselves in the same city, so if it happened on this occasion it is reasonable to suppose that it happened on others. However, intimacy between members of different embassies could go too far. This was the charge levelled against Timagoras, one of the Athenian ambassadors sent to King Artaxerxes in 367, by Leon, one of his colleagues. 'Timagoras had failed to share quarters with him and had taken counsel with Pelopidas [the Theban mission's leader] in all matters,' writes Xenophon.[69] On returning to Athens, where he was also accused of accepting extravagant Persian bribes, Timagoras paid the ultimate price.

Treaties

The treaties of ancient Greece were made for many purposes, among them facilitating the commercial dealings of citizens of one state in another (*symbolai*); and providing for arbitration (see Chapter 3), neutrality, non-aggression, the formation of military

---

[64] The Argives empowered 12 men to conduct these negotiations, Thucydides, *Peloponnesian War*, p. 325 [5.27.2-28.1].
[65] Adcock and Mosley, *Diplomacy in Ancient Greece*, p. 168.
[66] For example, the conference at Athens called by the Athenians of all those inclined to ratify the King's Peace of 387.
[67] Such was the Athenian embassy sent in pursuit of one from Thebes to the Persian court in 367, Xenophon, *Hellenika*, 7.1.33.
[68] Thucydides, *Peloponnesian War*, p. 330 [5.36.1].
[69] Xenophon, *Hellenika*, 7.1.38.

alliances (*symmachia*, see Chapter 3), and the making of peace at the end of a war. Although hybrids were by no means rare,[70] peace treaties were generally of two kinds:

- The bilateral peace treaty that was usually time limited and – although containing provisions on territorial matters for example – in practice was little more than a long truce, anything up to 100 years. These were characteristic of the fifth century, when it was still assumed that war was the normal relationship between city-states. The so-called Thirty Years' Peace agreed by Athens and Sparta in 446/5 was a peace treaty of this sort.

- The 'common peace' (*koine eirene*): a multilateral agreement to which, ideally, all Greek city-states were parties, recognised the autonomy and equality of them all irrespective of their military power, and were intended to remain in force for ever. It was less clear on how this should be enforced because 'autonomy' also signified the right to use force, and in practice it relied on a hegemon.[71] This idea of a peace treaty began to take hold imperfectly in the fourth century, beginning with the King's Peace of 387/6, and is perhaps evidence of a significant cooling in attitudes to the normality of war.[72]

If securing a treaty was the task of an embassy and if this were to be achieved, it was sealed not by the 'signature' of a plenipotentiary, in the modern manner, but – as actually spelled out in the Peace of Nicias in 421 – by the public exchange of oaths in the name of gods most respected and feared by each party. Treaties themselves, the terms of which were sometimes repeated in oaths, were actually described as oaths (*horkoi*). The oaths were sworn by key figures in each state in the presence of embassies from the other party to the treaty and it may be that each had the right to nominate who should swear these oaths in the other state.[73] Clearly it would have made sense to pin down by this means those with the greatest ability to keep or break the treaty. In a democracy the administering of oaths by an embassy was usually preceded by confirmation of the treaty's terms by the popular assembly, as is often the case today. This was the procedure followed in Athens in regard to the Peace of Philocrates negotiated by the first embassy

---

[70] For example, a 'peace treaty' could also set up a new alliance, as in the case of the Peace of Philocrates, which stipulated that Athens should become an ally of Philip of Macedon; and a multilateral alliance could contain elements of a 'common peace'.

[71] Although the concept of 'collective security', fundamental to the League of Nations and the UN in the twentieth century, surfaced in the proposal for an alliance-style duty of mutual assistance in a common peace unsuccessfully advanced by Athens in 371, Perlman, 'Greek diplomatic tradition', pp. 161-2.

[72] On the imperfect application of this idea in and following the King's Peace, see the clear and authoritative *Wikipedia* article, 'Common Peace'; also, Adcock and Mosley, *Diplomacy in Ancient Greece*, pp. 221-2.

[73] This is speculated in Adcock and Mosley, where also the complications attending the administering of oaths for a multilateral agreement are explained, *Diplomacy in Ancient Greece*, pp. 219-21.

to Philip of Macedon. The assembly having voted its approval, oaths were then sworn before Philip's ambassadors in Athens and envoys thereafter despatched to Macedon to receive his own oaths, which were duly given – although it suited him to delay the ceremony.

The terms of a treaty were usually inscribed by each party on a stone or bronze pillar (*stele*); 'the firmest guarantee that such agreements will hold good,' wrote Diodorus the Sicilian, 'is the certainty provided by a written text.'[74] These *stelai* were placed in the temples of the treaty parties, sometimes also at sacred locations elsewhere. Thus the Peace of Nicias of 421 prescribed in one of its clauses that it should be announced in this fashion not only on the Athenian Acropolis (the most common place for inscription of Athenian treaties, where the temple known as the Parthenon was dedicated to the goddess Athena) and in the Spartan temple at Amyclae but also at the religious sites at Olympia, Pythia (Delphi), and the Isthmus.[75] This was clearly another way of warning anyone contemplating breach of a treaty that such an act would invite divine retribution. The oaths confirming the Peace of Nicias, which was to last for 50 years, were also to be renewed annually. Treaty-*stelai* were sometimes destroyed when the treaties they recorded expired or were dishonoured, as in the case of the Athenian *stele* bearing the Peace of Philocrates, urged by Demosthenes to have been breached by Philip of Macedon. But this was rare, a fact which underlined the importance attached to their religious function.

Many alliances and peace settlements, such as the Peace of Nicias, lapsed after only a few years but this was often because of a change of regime in one or other party or because they were negotiated for reasons of the moment rather than as insurance policies against an uncertain future[76] – not because they had been carelessly contrived. Some peace treaties also survived for their full terms; for example, those of Sparta with Argos in 451/0 and with Mantinea in 418/7, both for 30 years.[77] And some very important ones that did not last their full terms at least had a substantial life. For example, the Thirty-Year Peace that ended the First Peloponnesian War lasted for almost half of its time. Breaches in individual treaty provisions were also common but – provided they were not major – did not necessarily lead to the termination of the treaty as a whole. The city-states obviously regarded treaties as valuable otherwise they would not have bothered to negotiate them in the first place, and they did not relish being thought contemptuous of the gods by being seen to be wilfully breaking them. Agreements made with non-Greek ('barbarian') states were also to be honoured.

---

[74]   Diodorus Siculus, *The Persian Wars*, p. 103.
[75]   For the full text, see 'Peace of Nicias'.
[76]   Adcock and Mosley, *Diplomacy in Ancient Greece*, pp. 136-7, 222-6, 231ff.
[77]   Adcock and Mosley, *Diplomacy in Ancient Greece*, p. 137.

Further reading

Rhetoric

Adcock, Sir Frank and D. J. Mosley, *Diplomacy in Ancient Greece* (Thames and Hudson: London, 1975)

Duke, George, 'The Sophists (Ancient Greek)', *Internet Encyclopedia of Philosophy*, available online.

Nicolson, Harold, *The Evolution of Diplomatic Method* (Constable: London, 1954)

Rapp, Christof, 'Aristotle's Rhetoric', *The Stanford Encyclopedia of Philosophy*, Spring 2010, Edward N. Zalta (ed.) [www].

Wardman, A., *Rome's Debt to Greece* (Duckworth: London, 2002), Ch. 5 (Rhetoric)

Private negotiations

Westlake, H. D., 'Diplomacy in Thucydides', *Bulletin of the John Rylands Library*, vol. 53, 1970-1

Rung, Edward, 'War, peace and diplomacy in Graeco-Persian relations from the sixth to the fourth century BC', in Philp de Souza and John France (eds), *War and Peace in the Ancient World* (Cambridge University Press: Cambridge, 2008)

Treaties

Adcock, Sir Frank and D. J. Mosley, *Diplomacy in Ancient Greece* (Thames and Hudson: London, 1975), Ch. 17

Badian, E., 'The Peace of Callias', *The Journal of Hellenic Studies*, vol. 107, 1987

Bolmarcich, Sarah, 'The afterlife of a treaty', *Classical Quarterly*, vol. 57 (2), December 2007

'Common Peace', *Wikipedia* [www]. This is a clear and authoritative exercise in history of ideas and diplomatic history, based largely on German sources.

Gardner, P. and F. B. Jevons, *A Manual of Greek Antiquities* (Scribner's: New York, 1895), Ch. 22 [www].

'Peace of Nicias', Livius.org [www]. This includes the text of the peace treaty and of the defensive alliance signed by Athens and Sparta in the same year.

Perlman, S., 'Greek diplomatic tradition and the Corinthian League of Philip of Macedon', *Historia: Zeitschrift für Alte Geschichte*, Bd. 34, H. 2, 1985

Phillipson, Coleman, *The International Law and Custom of Ancient Greece and Rome*, vol. I (Macmillan: London, 1911), Ch. 15 [www].

Rhodes, P. J., 'Making and breaking treaties in the Greek world', in Philp de Souza and John France (eds), *War and Peace in the Ancient World* (Cambridge University Press: Cambridge, 2008)

Sommerstein, A. H. and A. J. Bayliss, *Oath and State in Ancient Greece* (De Gruyter: Berlin and Boston, 2013), Part 2 ('Oaths and Interstate Relations', by Bayliss)

3   Multilaterals

The multilateral diplomacy of ancient Greece was extensive and extremely important.
Some of it took place in ad hoc conferences such as the peace congress at Delphi
in 368. Arranged at the behest of Philiscus, vice-regent of the rebellious Persian
satrap, Ariobarzanes, the chief parties here were the Thebans and their allies and the
Lacedaemonians. But it surely occurred to a greater extent in the states-system's religious
leagues and large-member military alliances (or 'leagues'), the last of which were usually
temporary arrangements made for joint action with a specific end in view and were
not designed to establish states.[78] The religious leagues were the earliest to appear but
the alliances were diplomatically by far the most important. International arbitration
was also of significance in the ancient Greek system and is considered in this chapter
because, by definition, it consisted in the intervention of a third party. The chapter
concludes with a lingering glance at the Panhellenic public festivals, events that are
normally remembered for reasons remote from diplomacy.

Religious leagues

The religious leagues, or amphictyonies ('dwellers around the temple'), were originally
associations of neighbouring communities sharing a deity which, in their religious
observance and exchanging of goods, naturally gravitated to the sanctuary of a
conveniently situated shrine. The maintenance and defence of the shrine, together with
the preservation of harmony between members, were the most important duties of
each amphictyony. Those who broke the obligatory oaths underpinning either of these
commitments precipitated at the least a fine and at the most a savage reprisal by the
other members, a 'sacred war'.[79]

There was certainly an amphictyony based at the sanctuary of the temple of
Apollo on the island of Delos that was well established by the early part of the seventh

---

[78]   I exclude from consideration here the numerous federal and confederal states of ancient Greece –
although the formation of some was preceded by a military alliance – because it would hardly be
right to describe the relations between their members as 'diplomatic'. It is misleading that so many
of these *states* are still called 'leagues', since this term is also widely used for military alliances – in
the same way that the Greeks applied the term *koinon* (community) to them all. Thus the following
have been authoritatively described by Hans Beck as the chief 'federal states' of ancient Greece: the
Boeotian *League*, the Thessalian *League*, the Aetolian *League*, the Achaean *League*, and the short-
lived Arcadian *League*, Beck, 'Federal states', pp. 294-5.

[79]   The so-called 'First Sacred War', said to have been launched about 590 by an early incarnation of the
Delphic Amphictyony and to have resulted in the destruction of the impious city of 'Crisa', has been
convincingly demonstrated to be a fiction devised by the supporters of Philip of Macedon to justify
his intervention in the 'Third' Sacred War, Robertson, 'The Myth of the First Sacred War'.

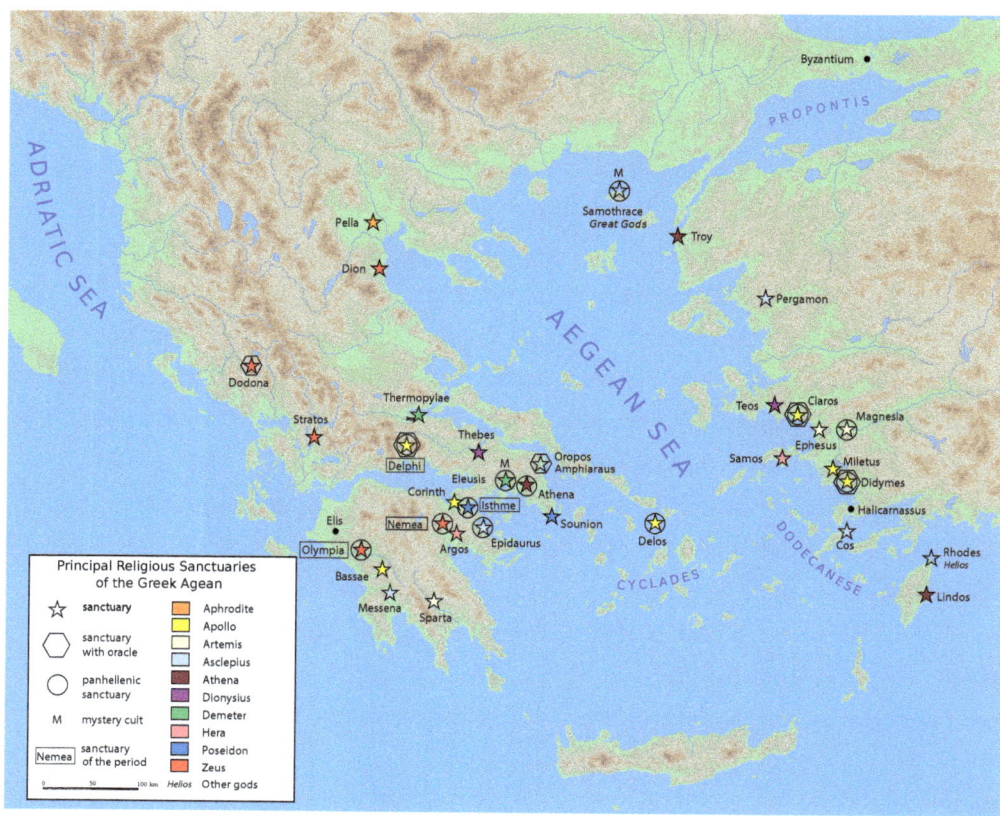

The main sanctuaries of Classical Greece

century; also one at Onchestus, and probably others at Argos and Corinth and many additional places to which there is no record of the technical term being applied. By far the most famous and important, however, was the Delphic Amphictyony, which also honoured Apollo (Box 3.1). The prestige of the 'Great Amphictyony' was reinforced by its legendary oracle, the pronouncements of which were usually treated with great respect by those who consulted it – not least because its role gave its priesthood 'unique opportunities of collecting foreign intelligence.'[80] But not everyone did. The political influence of the Delphic Oracle was limited chiefly to Western Greece, and it was only occasionally – in the fourth century – consulted by Athens. It played little role in arbitration, no doubt because its methods were suspect: it employed no tribunal, held no inquiry and heard no witnesses. And, describing the conference at Delphi mentioned at the beginning of this chapter, Xenophon tells us drily that the Greeks 'did not consult the god at all about how to make peace but instead discussed it among themselves.'[81]

---

[80] 'Oracle', *Encyclopedia Britannica*.
[81] Xenophon, *Hellenika*, Book 7.1.27.

> **Box 3.1 The Delphic Amphictyony**
>
> Like its Delian counterpart, the Delphic Amphictyony, or 'Great Amphictyony', seems also to have been established in the Archaic period of ancient Greek history. It was at first composed only of twelve tribes of north-eastern Greece in which Thessaly was the most influential member. The others were the Boeotians, Dorians, Ionians, Perrhaebians, Magnetes, Locrians, Oetaeans, Phthiotes, Malians, Phocians, and Dolopians. Its focal point was initially the temple of Demeter at Anthela, near Thermopylae, the sanctuary of Apollo at Delphi being added only later, although this became much the most important.
>
> The association's principal body was a council that met each year in spring and autumn. It consisted of deputies of two kinds. The senior were nominally the *hieromnemones*, two for each tribe holding office for a year. However, being usually appointed by lot, they were often of low ability and little if any experience of public affairs. The consequence was that the second kind of deputy, the *pylagorae* (two for each of the hieromnemones), actually commanded far more influence in the council's deliberations than their 'delegation leader', the reason for this being that they were elected and, in consequence, were orators and statesmen. Matters of special importance had to be approved by an assembly. This consisted of the deputies themselves, the amphictyonic priests, and any other citizens of the association who happened to be present; but this seems to have been little more than a rubber-stamping affair. Sometimes the council took up 'the Hellenic cause' but the association never acquired universal religious authority within the states-system of which it was a part.
>
> Athens, Macedon, Thebes, and the Aetolians subsequently elbowed their way into the Delphic Amphictyony, either via formal membership or control of existing members. As a result, although no member state had a formal veto over important decisions, from time to time it became a vehicle for the policies of the greatest power of the day. For example, in the third century the Aetolians were able effectively to convert the council into an organ of their own league. In such circumstances it would surely have collapsed had it not been for the bond of religion. In the event, it survived until the second century AD.

It is true that the nominal rationale of the religious leagues was wholly religious but it is inherently implausible that, at a time when there was no 'clear division between the secular and the religious',[82] they had no political underbelly. Another reason for this is that oratory was as important at the councils of the amphictyonies as it was in the political relations between city-states. The consequence was that the same statesmen were often active in both. Aeschines, whom we met in Chapter 1, is a well-known example, at one time serving as an elected representative of Athens in the Delphic Amphictyony. In any case, it is firmly established that such bodies tended to become the diplomatic tools of the more powerful military states (Box 3.1). Furthermore, in the event of a decision by the amphictyony to commence a 'sacred war' against a delinquent member, it would have been essential for a council to debate its political implications and negotiate on the division of labour and strategy of the operation. It would also be naïve to assume that private conversations between delegations were any less common in the wings of such meetings than they were between embassies and their hosts, as argued in Chapter 2.

Military alliances

Military alliances (*symmachia*) were established either for defence or – far more often – for defence and offense. When multilateral they were typically led by the most powerful

---

[82]   Adcock and Mosley, *Diplomacy in Ancient Greece*, p. 229.

member, or hegemon. They were confirmed by treaties (see Chapter 2). Most were short-lived but a few lasted for long periods and had an enormous impact on the history of ancient Greece. Notable among these interstate associations were those led by Sparta, Athens, and Macedon.

The Spartan-dominated Peloponnesian League, known at the time as 'the Lacedaemonians and their allies', was more loosely organized than its Athenian rivals although in practice not so different. It lasted from the middle of the sixth century until 366 and, like other such institutions, was held together by bilateral treaties between the leading power and its allies rather than by anything resembling a founding 'constitution'; neither did it have a council or bureaucracy. Conferences of the league, which were rare, were held on an ad hoc basis as and when occasion demanded; for example, in order to debate and vote on motions to declare war or the proposed terms and procedures for arranging a peace settlement. They usually met in Sparta but only when they were summoned, and there is no evidence – and no convincing reason to suppose – that Sparta was under any obligation either to call for a vote or bow to a majority of which it was not a part. On the other hand, it sometimes found it prudent to consult its allies because the league was 'fractious'; besides, collectively they contributed 'the lion's share of the League's military strength.'[83] But even when the Spartans did support a vote, which was expressed by shouting, this was usually designed to intimidate their allies into endorsing its favoured course of action. Since it did not formally highlight power differentials, this loose form of alliance probably had the advantage of not rubbing the noses of the lesser allies in their individual weakness whilst reducing any loss of face on the part of Sparta when it found it expedient to yield to their combined opposition, as on the occasion of its late sixth century proposal to re-impose a tyrant on Athens.

As for the Athens-led military alliances, the first was a naval alliance composed chiefly of the Ionian Greek cities located around the Aegean Sea and on its many islands. It was founded in 478/7 in order to consolidate the repulse of the invasion of Greece by the Persians a few years earlier and go onto the offensive against them in the Aegean Sea and western Asia Minor, later in the eastern Mediterranean. But it was essentially 'a pact of mutual assistance against *all* possible enemies' and from the beginning also had an anti-Sparta edge.[84] Because the sanctuary of Apollo on Delos was venerated by the Ionian Greeks, as well as because the island occupied a central position in the Aegean, it was chosen by the alliance as its base, and in consequence came to be known by modern scholars as the Delian League.[85] The total number of its members has always been

---

[83] Lendon, 'Thucydides and the 'Constitution' of the Peloponnesian League', p. 171.

[84] Lendering, 'Delian League'. Sparta, although prominent in the Persian war, held aloof from the new league.

[85] It is also known as the 'First Athenian Confederation'. In ancient sources it is described simply – and more accurately – as 'the alliance' or 'Athens and its allies', Cartwright, 'Delian League'.

The Delian League ('Athenian Empire') in 431

difficult to calculate but possibly exceeded 200; from this membership the Athenians did not brook desertions.

Unlike the Peloponnesian League, the Delian League had a council (*synod*) and a common treasury. As well as discussing contributions of ships and money, the league's council also had before it matters such as the suppression of piracy in the Aegean. Allied members had equal voting rights on the council, although Athens invariably got its way because of its great prestige acquired in fighting the Persians and because the many small states were afraid to vote against it. Furthermore, the council did not sit in permanent session and representatives from its wide membership could not be summoned quickly to debate a policy requiring urgent action.[86] The Athenians also appointed the board of ten officials charged with looking after the league's funds, which in 454 they removed to their own city. The role of Athens relative to the Delian League was clearly analogous to that of the United States to NATO, and it was not so many years before the body came to

---

[86] The alliance with Argos formed hurriedly by Athens in the 460s in fear of Spartan hostility, seems for this reason not to have been brought before the council. This might not have been the only reason, however, because Argos had been neutral in the Persian wars and an Athenian proposal of an alliance with it might, therefore, have been met with a distinctly cool response from the eastern Greeks, Powell, *Athens and Sparta*, pp. 36-8.

be little more than window-dressing for an Athenian empire. The council slowly lost its importance, had probably ceased to exist by 432 and, following defeat at the hands of the Spartans in the Peloponnesian War, the league itself was wound up in 404.

> **Box 3.2   The Decree of Aristoteles, 377**
>
> This famous decree, passed by the Athenian assembly on the proposal of the statesman, Aristoteles, listed the existing members of the recently established Second Athenian League, described its purpose, and invited others to join, including any 'barbarians' (non-Greeks) on the mainland or islands not subjects of Persia. Despite the fact that the decree was evidently conceived as a prospectus, it is sometimes described as the founding 'charter' of the League. A key clause, making clear its purely defensive character, stated that: *'If anybody attacks those who have made the alliance, either by land or by sea, the Athenians and the allies shall support the latter both by land and by sea with all their strength as far as possible.'*
>
> A translation by Stephen Lambert and P. J. Rhodes (from which the above clause is drawn), together with very useful annotations, can be found at 'Attic Inscriptions Online' [www]. The decree was inscribed on a stone *stele*. Images of the reconstructed fragments of this can be seen in Christopher A. Baron's 'The Aristoteles decree and the expansion of the Second Athenian League', *Hesperia*, vol. 75 (3), July-September 2006 [www].

The Second Athenian League was a defensive alliance created in 378/7. Its purpose was to guard against a growing fear that Sparta would not honour the 'common peace' provisions of the King's Peace on the autonomy of the Greek cities;[87] later, Thebes became the main threat. It began with a number of bilateral treaties made by Athens, first with Chios, and swelled to a membership that rose to over 70 city-states, a large proportion of which were former members of the Delian League. Each new member affirmed its alliance with the allies of Athens as well as with Athens itself. Its growth was assisted by Athenian propaganda in the shape of the Decree of Aristoteles (see Box 3.2). This time, however, an attempt was made to remove those features of the Delian League that had transformed it into an Athenian empire. Among these was a formal change in the new league's decision-making procedures. Like the Delian League, it had a council (*synedrion*) composed of delegations of the members, which each had one vote. But, although it met in Athens itself, rather than Delos – thereby tacitly acknowledging Athenian leadership – Athens had neither membership of the council nor presiding authority at its frequent meetings. Instead, its own council was nominally just the equal of the allies' council in matters of joint concern. To the extent that the league had a constitution, therefore, it was a 'bi-cameral' one. In practice, however, the allies' council was analogous to what today we would call an advisory council, an official body on which sit the representatives of interest groups with an acknowledged right to convey their views to the executive authority. The council does appear to have had real influence on some matters, particularly the admission of new members and re-admission of old ones. But, in part no doubt because it was seated permanently in Athens and its members were therefore continuously subject to the city's atmosphere and informal pressures, it

---

[87]   On the King's Peace, see Xenophon, *Hellenika*, 5.1.29-33; 'King's Peace', *Oxford Classical Dictionary*.

seems likely that on great issues its impact was not great. While acknowledging that the evidence on procedure is 'partial and confusing', Tuplin judges the likelihood to be that the allies were 'generally manipulated or sidelined.'[88] The Second Athenian League began to crumble in the mid-350s because the imperial reflexes of Athens could be suppressed no more than could the hostile reaction to them of its proud allies; hence 'the Social War'. But it managed to survive until 338/7, when, following the decisive defeat of Athens and Thebes by Philip II of Macedon at the battle of Chaeronea, its members were absorbed by the king into the awesome League of Corinth. In part to avoid gratuitous humiliation of the Greeks, this was modelled on the hegemonial alliance of Greek diplomatic tradition, with at least one important procedural difference. This is that an element of weighted voting in the council of allies was introduced – each member to have votes reflecting the size of its military contribution to the planned war against Persia. This would flatter the former great powers such as Athens and economize on the effort needed to garner votes.[89]

Interstate arbitration[90]

Following the outbreak of a quarrel between states, whether internal to one league or not, a call for 'arbitration' was a common reflex of the Greek cities, and testified particularly well to the cultural solidarity of their world emphasised in the Introduction to this book. Arbitration meant allowing judgment on a dispute to be passed by an impartial third party, which is why I treat it as an institution of the *multilateral* diplomacy of the Greek system.

By far the most common of the arbitrated disputes involving states were those of a territorial nature: who had rightful possession of a territory or – much the same thing – where precisely did a frontier run. This was partly because fertile land with good irrigation was not abundant and because transport routes, strategic positions, and natural resources all boiled down to the question of territory. Among other arbitrated disputes were unpaid debts and rights over shrines; sometimes arbitrators were even required to pronounce on *all* matters in dispute between two states. But before the middle of the fifth century (it might have been earlier) 'the dispute arose first and then the means of settlement were proposed.'[91] Afterwards, there was a significant change: important treaties sometimes began to provide that any *future* disputes over their clauses –irrespective of their subject – should be referred to arbitration. The first treaty known to be of this sort was the Thirty Years' Peace between Athens and Sparta concluded in the winter of 446-5.

---

[88]   Tuplin, 'Second Athenian Confederacy'.
[89]   Adcock and Mosley, *Diplomacy in Ancient Greece*, pp. 244-5; see also Perlman, 'Greek diplomatic tradition', p. 155. This claim is disputed by others.
[90]   Except where otherwise specified, this section draws heavily on Tod, *International Arbitration* and Ager, *Interstate Arbitrations*.
[91]   Adcock and Mosley, *Diplomacy in Ancient Greece*, p. 210.

Although supplying arbitrators could be costly and time-consuming and was not without risk, city-states willing to provide the service were not difficult to obtain.[92] This is chiefly because – as in later ages down to the modern day – great prestige was to be won by a third party invited to help resolve a dispute, the more so should its efforts be rewarded with success. As a result, even unsolicited offers of arbitration were by no means rare.[93] The important island state of Rhodes acquired a considerable reputation for successful arbitration in the latter part of the Hellenistic period, rather in the manner of Algeria in the late twentieth century AD, and rarely seems to have been shy to offer its services.

Sometimes states asked a foreign citizen with fame for wisdom and fairness to arbitrate in their disputes. Most often, however, they chose a state – usually one of great prestige, not too remote, and to which there were ties of kinship. In the Hellenistic age, the last two desiderata notwithstanding, the great kings were popular. In the interests of producing a verdict that would command maximum respect – as both in modern day international courts and the 'contact groups' that made a strong mark in international mediation in the late twentieth century AD – it was also known for a tribunal to consist of judges from a number of different states (Box 3.3). Whether the tribunal was held in the arbitrator's home state, in one of the disputing states, or on neutral territory, it frequently met at a sanctuary, not least because it was there that the obligatory oaths had most resonance. The character and size of the arbitral tribunal was usually left to the state supplying it.

Box 3.3 The Melitaea-Narthakion arbitration, ca. 143: a multistate tribunal

The small Thessalian cities of Melitaea and Narthakion had a long-running border dispute involving land on which certain temples were also located, the Melitaeans claiming that it was rightfully theirs but had been taken from them by their avaricious neighbour. As a result, two arbitrations were held in the fourth century, one conducted by Medeios of Larisa and the other by the Thessalians; one in the third century, held by the Macedonians; and another in the early part of the second century, once more presided over by the Thessalian League. The first three found in favour of Melitaea and the fourth in favour of Narthakion but on each occasion the unfavoured party evidently refused to accept the judgment. Perhaps it was in despair on the part of the Thessalian League at this situation that, around the middle of the second century, it either encouraged or required the disputants not only to look further afield for arbitrators but also to multiply their number. In any event, the agreement of three Greek states from Roman-controlled Asia Minor – Samos, Kolophon, and Magnesia – was duly acquired, each sending two judges. Whether they voted as individuals or as state blocs is not clear but, whatever the procedure, the tribunal smiled once more on the Narthakians. Unfortunately, the multistate tribunal method was no more successful and only a few years later, presumably because of Melitaean obduracy, this 'eternal dispute' was taken to Rome, where, unusually, it was heard – but not pondered in its details – by the Senate itself. No doubt impatient, this told the Greeks to accept the judgment of the Thessalian League; that is to say, to favour Narthakion.

---

[92] Tribunals of the more 'popular' sort could have memberships running into the hundreds, although these normally met in their home state. Those consisting only of 'experts', which were much better suited to site inspections, were far smaller, probably consisting of only three to five members.

[93] Mack, *Proxeny and Politics*, pp. 263-4.

In ancient Greece, arbitration was – as it has been ever since – in principle akin to judicial settlement, and normal court procedure was generally followed: the rival litigants presented their cases (accompanied by documents), witnesses were examined, the judges pronounced their verdict, and the litigants were obliged to accept it, whether they liked it or not. But in the Greek system it is clear that 'arbitration' was very often mediation by another name. There were two reasons for this.

First, mediation by a state anxious to see a settlement to a dispute was often necessary to get the fractious parties to agree to go to arbitration in the first place. This is because – aside from the fact that it was usually only the weaker party that favoured the procedure – acceptance of arbitration was inevitably conditional on securing an arbitrator satisfactory to both sides. Other conditions also had to be agreed; for example, that the precise limits of the subject be clear, that a verdict would not be too long delayed, that the arbitrators should visit in person the territory in dispute, that credible guarantees of fulfilment of the verdict would be provided, that suitable fines would be imposed on any defaulter, and so on. Stipulated in a preliminary agreement, these conditions were best publicised in order to commit both the parties and the arbitrator to them.[94] By the time that agreement to arbitration had been reached, therefore, any mediator required had already done much of the heavy lifting en route to a settlement.

Second, mediation often entered again when the tribunal's formal proceedings had reached a decision. Thus, instead of handing this down as a judicial verdict, which would have invited gloating on the part of the victor and openly humiliated the loser, the 'arbitrators' instead encouraged them quietly to accept what they suggested was a fair resolution of the dispute – what our own age would call an 'out of court settlement'. The great advantage of this was that, when possible, it was not only much more likely to gain acceptance of the decision but also restore good relations in general between the disputants and avoid threatening relations between the losing party and the arbitrating state as well.

Interstate arbitration in ancient Greece did not, as might be expected, have a record of untrammelled success, especially in settling conflicts between major alliances such as those led by Athens and Sparta in the Peloponnesian War. While potential arbitrators were always to be found, settling on one acceptable to two powerful parties with many allies was extremely difficult. On those occasions when it was sought by a powerful state, sometimes this seems to have been a ruse to gain the moral ascendancy prior to starting a war. Arbitration was more popular with smaller states, which had fewer options, As for the enforcement of judgments, even powerful arbitrators hesitated over this. Nevertheless, it is evident that a very large number of disputes in ancient

---

94   Publication is attested in some cases but whether this was customary is not clear.

Greece – in far from trivial cases – were referred to arbitration and that most verdicts were accepted by both parties. The example in Box 3.3 in a way proves this rule, for it shows that over more than two centuries of one or other disputant not getting the 'right' result, they did not give up on arbitration. Furthermore, employment of arbitration surely became more widespread during the fourth century, as experience with it accumulated and more attention generally was given to safeguards against war; and in the following century it played 'a very prominent part in Greek history.'[95] This is in large part because the arbitration of the ancient Greeks was less legalistic than that of our own day and because it was favoured by the Macedonian conquerors as a useful device for helping to keep the home front quiet while they concentrated on furthering their ambitions in more far-flung places.

Panhellenic public festivals

Panhellenic public festivals held to honour the gods and inspire competition in drama, music, poetry and above all – to the disgust of Isocrates – athletics, were a very important feature of life in ancient Greece.[96] With the stage set by processions and sacrifices, high prestige was to be won by those who excelled on these spectacular occasions, and valuable gifts and privileges were presented to the victors on returning home. But, on the side, they also made a significant contribution to multilateral diplomacy.

Among the greatest of these festivals were the four Panhellenic games, which – so that they did not clash – were held at different junctures in a four-year cycle, the *periodos*.[97] Staged every four years were the Olympic Games and the Pythian Games, the former held in honour of Zeus at the sanctuary of Olympia in Elis in the north-western Peloponnese and the latter for Apollo at Delphi. Held biennially were the Isthmian Games and the Nemean Games, the former taking place every two years on the supremely accessible Isthmus of Corinth, the site of much the most important of the festivals dedicated to the sea god, Poseidon; and the latter at the sanctuary of the same name to Zeus in the north-east of the Peloponnese, later in Argos. There were also rather more local festivals, among them the 'Great Panathenaia', a set of games added every four years to the annual festival held in Athens in honour of the goddess Athena; the Dionysian festival, held annually also in Athens; Laconia's Hyacinthia, which was marked particularly by the Spartans and the Amyclaeans at Amyclae; and the 'mysteries'

[95] Tod, *International Arbitration*, p. 180; see also Bozeman, *Politics and Culture in International History*, pp. 81-5.
[96] Isocrates, *Panegyricus*, 4.41.
[97] This is explained fully in Remijsen and Clarysse, 'The periodos'.

of the mythical Persephone and her mother Demeter, celebrated at Eleusis in Attica, the 'lesser' every year and the 'greater' every fourth.

All of these occasions were of some diplomatic significance because they were intervals of political truce in any conflict that happened to coincide with them, and in this regard resembled the funerals of leading political figures in the world diplomatic system over two thousand years later. But this was particularly true of the four major Panhellenic festivals, at which heralds called 'truce-bearers' were commonly sent out ahead of the opening ceremony to announce the 'sacred truce'; this lasted much longer than the games themselves in order to permit visitors to journey to and from them in safety. The truce of the five-day Olympiad, which in most respects was the model for the other games, endured for a full month. Any state breaching the truce might be given a hefty fine and, if it refused to pay, banned from the temple of the god and thus from taking part in the games. This was the predictable fate of the Spartans on the occasion of the Olympic Games in 420, when – claiming afterwards that news of the truce had not reached them – they made the elementary error of attacking a fort and an important city (Lepreum) belonging to none other than the event's organizers, the Elians.[98] As a rule, the sacred month was widely observed.

At the festivals, sacrifices to deities shared by friends as well as enemies were offered on the first day by special ambassadors sent by the attending states, while envoys were also given the tasks of presenting gifts to the sacred treasury and ensuring the display of 'copies, on tablets of stone or bronze, of treaties and decrees to which they wished to direct the eyes of all Greece.'[99] In his famous *Panegyricus*, Isocrates wrote of the diplomatic value of these festivals:

> Now the founders of our great festivals are justly praised for handing
> down to us a custom by which, having proclaimed a truce and resolved our
> pending quarrels, we come together in one place, where, as we make our
> prayers and sacrifices in common, we are reminded of the kinship which
> exists among us and are made to feel more kindly towards each other for the
> future, reviving our old friendships and establishing new ties.[100]

Isocrates was making the case for the advantages of the Greeks 'assembling together' the better to deal with the barbarian, as well as to assert the claim to leadership of Athens, which, as it happened, excelled in its festivals. So his suggestion that inter-state quarrels were almost automatically settled by diplomacy immediately prior to, during or following one of these occasions must be regarded with scepticism; his wish

---

[98] Thucydides, *History*, pp. 340-1 [5.48-51].
[99] Gardner and Jevons, *Manual*, p. 270.
[100] Isocrates, *Panegyricus*, 4.43.

was in any case too often father to this thought.[101] Nevertheless, he was right to point to their potential for stimulating and facilitating private contacts in the wings of these events (see also Box 2.1), and the fact that he saw it means it was likely that at least some others saw it too.

Further reading

Religious leagues
'Amphictyony', *Encyclopedia Britannica, 1911 edition* [George Willis Botsford] [www].

Boak, A. E. R., 'Greek interstate associations and the League of Nations', *The American Journal of International Law*, vol. 15 (3), July 1921[www].

Bonner, Robert J. and Gertrude Smith, 'Administration of justice in the Delphic Amphictyony', *Classical Philology*, 38 (1), January 1943

'Oracle', *Encyclopedia Britannica, 1911 edition* [L. R. Farnell] [www].

Military alliances
Boak, A. E. R., 'Greek interstate associations and the League of Nations', *The American Journal of International Law*, vol. 15 (3), July 1921 [www].

Cartwright, Mark, 'Delian League', *Ancient History Encyclopedia*, 4 March 2016 [www].

'Decree inviting states to join the Second Athenian League', 378/7BCE [Decree of Aristoteles], trsl. S. Lambert and P. J. Rhodes, *Attic Inscriptions Online*, RO22 [www].

'Delian League', *Encyclopedia Britannica, 1911 edition* [J. M. Mitchell] [www].

Kagan, Donald, *Pericles of Athens and the Birth of Democracy* (Secker and Warburg: London, 1990), Chs. 2 and 5

Lendering, Jona, 'Delian League', Livius.org 19 August 2017, [www].

Lendering, Jona, 'Peloponnesian League', Livius.org 19 June 2017 [www].

Lendon, J. E., 'Thucydides and the 'Constitution' of the Peloponnesian League', *Greek, Roman and Byzantine Studies*, vol. 35 (2), Summer 1994

'Peloponnesian War', *Encyclopedia Britannica, 1911 edition* [J. M. Mitchell] [www].

Perlman, S., 'Greek diplomatic tradition and the Corinthian League of Philip of Macedon', *Historia: Zeitschrift für Alte Geschichte*, Bd. 34, H. 2, 185

Planeaux, Christopher, 'The Delian League, Part 1: Origins down to the Battle of Eurymedon (480/79-465/4)', *Ancient History Encyclopedia*, 13 September 2016 [www].

Rhodes, P. J., 'Political leagues (other than Sparta's)' in Xenophon's *Hellenika*, App. H in Xenophon

Tuplin, C. J., 'Second Athenian Confederacy', *Oxford Classical Dictionary*, March 2016 [www].

Interstate arbitration
Ager, Sheila L., *Interstate Arbitrations in the Greek World, 337-90 B.C.* (University of California Press: Berkeley and London, 1996)

Tod, M. N., *International Arbitration amongst the Greeks* (Clarendon Press: Oxford, 1913) [www].

Westermann, W. L., 'Interstate arbitration in antiquity', *The Classical Journal*, vol. 2 (5), March 1907 [www].

---

[101] Romilly, 'Eunoia in Isocrates', p. 99.

Panhellenic public festivals

Adcock, Sir Frank and D. J. Mosley, *Diplomacy in Ancient Greece* (Thames and Hudson: London, 1975), pp. 199-200

Gardner, P. and F. B. Jevons, *A Manual of Greek Antiquities* (Scribner's: New York, 1895), Ch. 8 [www].

Remijsen, Sofie and Willy Clarysse, 'The periodos', *Ancient Olympics* [www].

4   Conclusion: Were the diplomatic methods of the ancient Greeks 'fit for purpose'?

The phrase 'fit for purpose' is now a cliché in the British political lexicon and makes me wince every time I hear it. But it has the advantage of highlighting the need to keep in mind the *purposes* of an institution in judging its effectiveness. This is particularly important in the case of diplomacy because the view is often heard that – negotiation being its chief activity – failure to keep the peace by this means is evidence of its ineffectiveness. Should this be true, the diplomacy of the ancient Greek city-states can immediately be dismissed as not fit for purpose, since war between them was a common occurrence even if not the normal characteristic of their relations. But while it is always possible that faulty diplomatic methods or use of suitable methods by incompetent persons might be the cause of war, at least to some degree, it must always be remembered that the instructions on which diplomats act are issued by political leaders. And such individuals might be resolved on war, or set their demands so high that their diplomats have no chance of getting them accepted; or, if more risk-averse, set their demands so low that their diplomats inevitably feed arrogance on the other side – all with the same result. In fact, war is usually a deliberate or accidental consequence of foreign policy, and for the winning side might well be evidence of the *effectiveness* of diplomacy if its personnel have been successful in solidifying alliances, negotiating base agreements, and securing the supply of strategic materials, all of which were vital to victory; and *effective for the losing side as well* if they were able to negotiate the best terms possible in a peace settlement. With such preliminary thoughts in mind, let us turn to the main question: Were the diplomatic methods of the ancient Greeks 'fit for purpose'; that is, for their commercial, cultural, foreign intelligence-gathering, and political/military purposes?

The city-states were clearly anxious for the development of trade not only in the Greek world but also beyond it. Although commerce was despised by the landed aristocrats who tended to hold sway even in the democracies, it was valued for obtaining essential supplies and for the revenues it generated from taxation, including poll taxes on the large number of transient and resident foreigners (*xenoi* and *metics*) amongst the traders. Long-distance trade expanded during the Classical period, for the traders 'took very little notice' of the wars,[102] and it became 'a specialized and important sector of the economy.'[103] This expansion would have been seriously hindered if not rendered

---

[102]   Michel, *Economics of Ancient Greece*, p. 229.
[103]   Engen, 'Economy of ancient Greece'.

impossible in the absence of diplomatic intervention: intervention to conclude treaties facilitating the commercial dealings of citizens of one state in another (especially *symbolai*, whereby foreign nationals were granted legal protection and equal status with citizens in the law courts[104]); to provide assistance (via *proxenoi*) to traders in difficulties; and to cultivate friendly relations with state-suppliers of vital goods and states adjacent to trade routes such as the Hellespont.

The ancient Greeks, as we know, were highly sensitive to their common culture but ethnic and political differences stood in the way of celebrating and enriching this in Panhellenic public festivals. These would have been seriously hindered if not rendered impossible in the absence of the sacred truce announced by heralds.

But were the diplomatic methods of the time also fit for the purpose of collecting foreign intelligence? Allegedly not: 'to the modern eye,' says one respected textbook, 'the diplomatic exchanges of the Greeks were marked by an astonishing ignorance.'[105] Another says that the collection of information was generally 'a haphazard affair' and cites some well-known cases of what today would be called intelligence failures, among them the surprise of the Greeks at the Theban defeat of Sparta at Leuctra in 371, and the ignorance of the Athenians about affairs in Sicily prior to the despatch of their ill-fated expedition to that large island in 415.[106] On the other hand, as we now know, even the smallest city-states had the eyes and ears of their *proxenoi* on foreign ground, many states were constantly sending abroad large embassies – which would hardly have had their own eyes shut and ears covered – and league councils and Panhellenic festivals must also have been fruitful grounds for obtaining intelligence. So it should not be surprising that there is abundant contrary evidence on the effectiveness of the diplomacy of the ancient Greeks and their 'barbarian' interlocutors in this role. Thus Philip of Macedon is reputed to have been able to discover 'within hours what his arch-opponent Demosthenes had said in his speeches in Athens,' and the Greeks themselves 'were often able to anticipate the moves of others in times of crisis' with 'unerring accuracy.' Among other things, this enabled them quickly to send a counter-embassy when they learned of the despatch of a mission by a rival to a third state.[107] The real problem was more with the absence of a system of bureaucratic storage and retrieval than with the collection of foreign intelligence, but the seriousness of this varied with the type of intelligence required and obtained. For example, while the recording of general intelligence on Sparta (size of citizen population, condition of army, mood of the helots, economic difficulties) would have been valuable to its enemies, the storage

---

[104] Michel, *Economics of Ancient Greece*, p. 227; see also Phillipson, *International Law and Custom*, pp. 139-40.
[105] Hamilton and Langhorne, *Practice of Diplomacy*, p. 15.
[106] Adcock and Mosley, *Diplomacy in Ancient Greece*, pp. 174-7.
[107] Adcock and Mosley, *Diplomacy in Ancient Greece*, p. 176.

of news of the despatch of an embassy by another city to Persia that required an instant response would have been irrelevant. When it is also borne in mind that little changed in wealth production and military technology in ancient Greece, that open diplomacy revealed so much, and that – at least for trading states such as Corinth, Rhodes and Athens – merchants were an additional source of foreign news, the diplomacy of the ancient Greeks was not at all badly set up for collecting the kind of intelligence required by the times.

Last but by no means least, there can be little doubt that the diplomacy of the ancient Greeks was fit for the purpose of negotiating agreements of a political and military kind, and then for underpinning them by oaths and publicity on *stelae*. The most important were chiefly peace settlements and military alliances – some of which were the building blocks of major leagues and included arbitration clauses – and these treaties were rarely transient even if it was unusual for them to last for their full terms. By such means the Greeks were able to join forces in resisting the assaults of Persia in the early fifth century and then to sustain a balance of power in the Aegean and the eastern Mediterranean that – notwithstanding a long interlude of Spartan 'hegemony' either side of the end of the century and a shorter one by Thebes later – lasted until the Macedonian conquest confirmed by the battle of Chaeronea in 338.

Nevertheless, echoing Demosthenes, Harold Nicolson – the most elegant and well-known writer on diplomacy in the English language in the twentieth century – complains that the democratic procedures of the Greeks placed them at a permanent diplomatic and military disadvantage in dealing with despotic regimes such as that of Philip of Macedon and that this contributed to this king's final victory over them at Chaeronea. Their decisions, he maintained, could 'never be either so secret or so quick,' or even so coherent.[108] This is certainly true.[109] But it is a condemnation of how foreign policy was made and ambassadors were handled, rather than of the diplomatic *methods* of the ancient Greeks – what sort of diplomatic agents they employed and what those agents actually did. In any case, in the 'perfect illustration' of the failings of 'democratic diplomacy' that he provides – the pre-Chaeronea Athenian bid to fire up Panhellenic resistance – Nicolson omits to notice, among half a dozen other things, that the Second Athenian League still provided some allies; that another diplomatic institution, proxeny, assisted Athens to enlist the critical assistance of hitherto hostile Thebes; and that the Greeks could well have won the day at Chaeronea against a lesser military leader than Philip II.[110] In so far as Nicolson criticized their diplomatic methods, his main target was

---

[108] Nicolson, *Evolution of Diplomatic Method*, p. 11: 'delays and *confusions* [were] inherent in democratic diplomacy' (emphasis added).

[109] See also Green, *Alexander the Great*, p. xix: 'The cumbersome democratic process met efficient autocracy and failed.'

[110] Demosthenes was *proxenos* of Thebes in Athens, and it was chiefly his personal diplomacy that

the 'mixed embassy', but this had advantages as well as disadvantages. He also makes no allowance for the extensive but little-remarked resort to private diplomacy that was also a feature of the Greek system, as we have seen;

Conditions in ancient Greece favoured an energetic diplomacy, as emphasised in the Introduction, but others imposed heavy handicaps on its mechanisms and gave them an excessive workload. An exceptional burden on both was the enormous number of city-states, which made agreement on matters of common concern more difficult to achieve, while their long peripheries relative to their area led to countless boundary disputes. In all of the circumstances, particularly these, the diplomacy of the ancient Greeks was remarkably effective, and certainly more so than might be concluded from a hasty reading of their recurring wars and occasional disposition to 'lay waste' to the countryside and level the city of a defeated rival. I am inclined to agree with Adam Watson that the ancient Greeks produced 'one of the most developed periods of diplomacy before our time.'[111]

---

persuaded the Thebans to stand with the Athenians at Chaeronea, Adcock and Mosley, *Diplomacy in Ancient Greece*, p. 96; see also, Demosthenes, 18.169-79. It is instructive to compare Nicolson's account of the pre-Chaeronea diplomacy with that of Ryder, 'Demosthenes and Philip II'.

[111] Watson, *Diplomacy*, p. 86.

Some important dates

480	Conventional start of 'Classical' Period, marked by end of Persian threat
478/7	Formation of Delian League
458	Outbreak of First Peloponnesian War
454	Delian League treasury moved to Athens
449	Peace of Callias between Athens and Persia
446/5	Thirty Years' Peace treaty (with arbitration clause) ends First Peloponnesian War
431	Outbreak of (Second) Peloponnesian War
429	Death of Pericles
423	Year's Truce between Athens and Sparta
421	Peace of Nicias in Peloponnesian War, and Athens-Sparta defensive alliance
418	Battle of Mantinea, at which Peloponnesian League defeats Athens and its new democratic allies in Peloponnese and Peace of Nicias in tatters
415	Athenian military expedition to Sicily
413	Catastrophic Athenian defeat in Sicily and Nicias executed Renewal of Peloponnesian War
411	Persians intervene in war
405	Artaxerxes succeeds to throne of Persia Spartan admiral, Lysander, destroys Athenian fleet at Aegospotami
404	Surrender of Athens to Sparta and winding up of Delian League
395	Death of Thucydides
394	Thebes and Athens form coalition against Sparta Outbreak of Corinthian War
387/6	The King's Peace/ Peace of Antalcidas between Sparta and Persia
382	Spartans seize Thebes
378/7	Second Athenian Confederacy established

377	Decree of Aristoteles
371	Thebes defeats Sparta at Leuctra, and subsequently sets up Arcadian League
370	Athens switches to Sparta's side
362	Battle of Mantinea, a re-match of Leuctra again won by the Thebans, but their leaders killed
356	Outbreak of war between Athens and Macedon
355	Outbreak of 'Third Sacred War', between Delphic League and Phocians
346	Peace of Philocrates: Philip II of Macedon imposes peace and alliance on Athens
338	Battle of Chaeronea, decisive victory of Philip II of Macedonia over Greek forces led by Athens and Thebes
338/7	Formation of League of Corinth
323	Death of Alexander the Great and conventional start of the 'Hellenistic' period

References

Adcock, Sir Frank and D. J. Mosley, *Diplomacy in Ancient Greece* (Thames and Hudson: London, 1975)

Aeschines, 'Against Ctesiphon', Perseus Digital Library [www].

Aeschines, 'On the Embassy', Perseus Digital Library [www].

Ager, Sheila L., *Interstate Arbitrations in the Greek World, 337-90 B.C.* (University of California Press: Berkeley and London, 1996)

'Amphictyony', *Encyclopedia Britannica, 1911 edition* [G. W. Botsford] [www].

Anderson, J. K., *Xenophon* (Bristol Classical Press: London, 2001)

Badian, E., 'The Peace of Callias', *The Journal of Hellenic Studies*, vol. 107, 1987

Baron, Christopher A., 'The Aristoteles decree and the expansion of the Second Athenian League', *Hesperia*, vol. 75 (3), July-September 2006 [www].

Beck, Hans, 'Federal states', *Encyclopedia of Ancient Greece*, ed. Nigel Wilson (Routledge: New York and London, 2006)

Berridge, G. R., *Diplomacy: Theory and Practice*, 5th ed (Palgrave Macmillan: Basingstoke, 2015)

Boak, A. E. R., 'Greek interstate associations and the League of Nations', *The American Journal of International Law*, vol. 15 (3), July 1921 [www].

Bolmarcich, Sarah, 'The afterlife of a treaty', *Classical Quarterly*, vol. 57 (2), December 2007

Bonner, Robert J. and Gertrude Smith, 'Administration of justice in the Delphic Amphictyony', *Classical Philology*, 38 (1), January 1943

Bozeman, Adda B., *Politics and Culture in International History: From the Ancient Near East to the Opening of the Modern Age*, 2nd ed (Transaction: New Brunswick and London, 1994)

Bruce, I. A. F., 'Athenian embassies in the early fourth century B.C.', *Historia*, 15 (3), August 1966

Buckler, John, 'Demosthenes and Aeschines', in Worthington, I. (ed), *Demosthenes: Statesman and orator* (Routledge: London and New York, 2000)

'Caduceus', *Encyclopedia Britannica, 1911 edition* [www].

Cartwright, Mark, 'Delian League', *Ancient History Encyclopedia*, 4 March 2016 [www].

Cartwright, Mark, 'Trade in ancient Greece', *Ancient History Encyclopedia*, 22 May 2018 [www].

Casson, Lionel, *Travel in the Ancient World* (Allen and Unwin: London, 1974)

'Common Peace', *Wikipedia* [www]. This is a clear and authoritative exercise in history of ideas and diplomatic history, based largely on German sources.

'Decree inviting states to join the Second Athenian League', 378/7BCE [Decree of Aristoteles], trsl. S. Lambert and P. J. Rhodes, *Attic Inscriptions Online*, RO22 [www].

'Delian League', *Encyclopedia Britannica, 1911 edition* [J. M. Mitchell] [www].

'Demosthenes', *Encyclopedia Britannica, 1911 edition* [R. C. Jebb] [www].

Demosthenes, 'On the Crown', 18.169-79, Perseus Digital Library [www].

Demosthenes, 'On the False Embassy', 19, Perseus Digital Library [www].

Diodorus Siculus: *The Persian Wars to the Fall of Athens: Books 11-14.34 (480-401 BCE)*, translated, with introduction and notes by Peter Green (University of Texas Press: Austin, 2010)

Diodorus Siculus, vols. 4-8, translated by C. H. Oldfather (Harvard University Press: Cambridge, Mass.; Heinemann: London, 1989. Perseus Digital Library [www].

Duke, George, 'The Sophists (Ancient Greek)', *Internet Encyclopedia of Philosophy* [www].

Engen, Darel, 'The Economy of Ancient Greece', EH.net Encyclopedia [Economic History Association], ed. Robert Whaples 31 July, 2004 [www].

'Ephor', *Encyclopedia Britannica, 1911 edition* [M. N. Tod] [www].

Frey, Linda S. and Marsha L. Frey, *The History of Diplomatic Immunity* (Ohio State University Press: Columbus, 1999)

Gagarin, M. and Fantham, E. (eds), *The Oxford Encyclopedia of Ancient Greece and Rome*, vol. 4 (Oxford University Press: Oxford, 2010)

Gardner, P. and F. B. Jevons, *A Manual of Greek Antiquities* (Scribner's: New York, 1895) [www].

Grant, J. R., 'A note on the tone of Greek diplomacy', *The Classical Quarterly*, New Series, 15 (2), November 1965

Green, Peter, *Alexander the Great and the Hellenistic Age: A short history* (Weidenfeld and Nicolson: London, 2007)

Hamilton, K. and R. Langhorne, *The Practice of Diplomacy: Its evolution, theory and administration*, 2nd ed (Routledge: London and New York, 2011)

Hansen, M. H., *Polis: An introduction to the ancient Greek city-state* (Oxford University Press: New York, 2006)

Herodotus, *The Histories*, translated by Robin Waterfield with an Introduction and Notes by Carolyn Dewald (Oxford University Press: Oxford and New York, 1998)
An earlier English translation available at online can be found in the Perseus Digital Library [www].

Isocrates, 'On the Peace', in *Isocrates*, with an English translation by George Norlin, vol. 2 (Heinemann: London; Putnam: New York, 1929). Perseus Digital Library [www].

Isocrates, 'Panegyricus', in *Isocrates*, with an English translation by George Norlin, vol. 1 (Heinemann: London; Putnam: New York, 1929). Perseus Digital Library [www].

Kagan, Donald, *Pericles of Athens and the Birth of Democracy* (Secker and Warburg: London, 1990)

Kent, Peter (ed), *The Oxford Companion to Ships and the Sea* (Oxford University Press: Oxford and New York, 1988)

'King's Peace', *Oxford Classical Dictionary* [www].

Kralli, Ionna, 'Athenian proxeny decrees'. Review of E. Culasso Gastaldi, *Le prossenie ateniesi del IV secolo a.C. Gli onorati asiatici* (2004), *The Classical Review*, vol. 56 (2), October, 2006

Lendering, Jona, 'Delian League', Livius.org 19 August 2017 [www].

Lendering, Jona, 'Peloponnesian League', Livius.org 19 June 2017 [www].

Lendon, J. E., 'Thucydides and the 'Constitution' of the Peloponnesian League', *Greek, Roman and Byzantine Studies*, vol. 35 (2), Summer 1994

Mack, William, *Proxeny and Polis: Institutional Networks in the Ancient Greek World* (Oxford University Press: 2015)

Michell, H., *The Economics of Ancient Greece* (Cambridge University Press: Cambridge, 1940)

Nicolson, Harold, *The Evolution of Diplomatic Method* (Constable: London, 1954)

'Oracle', *Encyclopedia Britannica, 1911 edition* [L. R. Farnell] [www].

'Peace of Nicias', Livius.org [www].

'Peloponnesian War', *Encyclopedia Britannica, 1911 edition* [J. M. Mitchell] [www].

Perlman, S., 'Greek diplomatic tradition and the Corinthian League of Philip of Macedon', *Historia: Zeitschrift für Alte Geschichte*, Bd. 34, H. 2, 1985

Phillipson, Coleman, *The International Law and Custom of Ancient Greece and Rome*, vol. I (Macmillan: London, 1911) [www].

Planeaux, Christopher, 'The Delian League, Part 1: Origins down to the Battle of Eurymedon (480/79-465/4)', *Ancient History Encyclopedia*, 13 September 2016 [www].

Plato, *The Republic*, trsl. H. D. P. Lee (Penguin Books: Harmondsworth, 1955)

Plutarch's Lives: The translation called Dryden's, rev. A. H. Clough (Athenaeum: London, 1905), vol. 3 ('Cimon')

Plutarch's Lives: The translation called Dryden's, rev. A. H. Clough (Athenaeum: London, 1905), vol. 3 ('Nicias')

Powell, Anton, *Athens and Sparta: Constructing Greek political and social history from 478 BC*, 2nd ed (Routledge: London and New York, 2001)

Pretzler, Maria, *Pausanias: Travel writing in Ancient Greece* (Duckworth: London, 2007)

Proxeny Networks of the Ancient World (a database of proxeny networks of the Greek city-states) [www].

Rapp, Christof, 'Aristotle's Rhetoric', *The Stanford Encyclopedia of Philosophy*, Spring 2010, Edward N. Zalta (ed.) [www].

Remijsen, Sofie and Willy Clarysse, 'Heralds and trumpeters', *Ancient Olympics* [www].

Remijsen, Sofie and Willy Clarysse, 'The periodos', *Ancient Olympics* [www].

Rhodes, P. J., 'Political leagues (other than Sparta's)', App. H in Xenophon, Strassler ed., see below.

Rhodes, P. J., 'Making and breaking treaties in the Greek world', in Philp de Souza and John France (eds), *War and Peace in the Ancient World* (Cambridge University Press: Cambridge, 2008)

Roberts, Jennifer T., *The Plague of War: Athens, Sparta, and the struggle for ancient Greece* (Oxford University Press: New York, 2017)

Robertson, Noel, 'The myth of the First Sacred War', *The Classical Quarterly*, 28 (1), 1978

Roebuck, Carl, 'The settlements of Philip II with the Greek states in 338 B.C.', *Classical Philology*, vol. 43 (2), April 1948

Romilly, Jacqueline de, 'Eunoia in Isocrates or the political importance of creating good will', *Journal of Hellenic Studies*, vol. 78, 1958

Rung, Edward, 'War, peace and diplomacy in Graeco-Persian relations from the sixth to the fourth century BC', in Philp de Souza and John France (eds), *War and Peace in the Ancient World* (Cambridge University Press: Cambridge, 2008)

Rung, Edward, 'The Mission of Philiscus to Greece in 369/8 B.C.', *Anabasis. Studia classica et orientalia*. vol. 4, 2014 [www].

Ryder, T. T. B., 'Demosthenes and Philip II', in Worthington, I. (ed), *Demosthenes: Statesman and orator* (Routledge: London and New York, 2000)

Sealey, R., *Demosthenes: A study in defeat* (Oxford University Press: New York, 1993)

Starr, Chester G., *The Influence of Sea Power on Ancient History* (Oxford University Press: New York and Oxford, 1989)

Thucydides, *History of the Peloponnesian War*, translated with an Introduction by Rex Warner (Penguin Books: Harmondsworth, 1954)

Thucydides, *The Landmark Thucydides: A Comprehensive Guide to the Peloponnesian War*, ed. Robert B. Strassler (Simon and Schuster: New York, 1998)

Thucydides, *The Peloponnesian War*, trsl. Richard Crawley (Dent: London, 1910). Perseus Digital Library [www].

Tod, M. N., *International Arbitration amongst the Greeks* (Clarendon Press: Oxford, 1913) [www].

Toynbee, Arnold, *The Greeks and their Heritages* (Oxford University Press: Oxford, 1981)

Tozer, Rev. Henry Fanshawe, *Lectures on the Geography of Greece* (John Murray: London, 1873)

Tuplin, C. J., 'Second Athenian Confederacy', *Oxford Classical Dictionary*, March 2016 [www].

Wallace, M. B., 'Early Greek *proxenoi*', *Phoenix*, vol. 24, 1970

Wardman. A., *Rome's Debt to Greece* (Duckworth: London, 2002)

Watson, A., *Diplomacy: The dialogue between states* (Eyre Methuen: London, 1982)

Westermann, W. L., 'Interstate arbitration in antiquity', *The Classical Journal*, vol. 2 (5), March 1907 [www].

Westlake, H. D., 'Diplomacy in Thucydides', *Bulletin of the John Rylands Library*, vol. 53, 1970-1

Wilamowitz-Moellendorff, Ulrich von, *Reden und Vorträge*, 3rd ed (Weidmann: Berlin, 1913)

Xenophon: Strassler, R. B. (ed.), *The Landmark Xenophon's Hellenika*, trsl. by J. Marincola Quercus: London, 2011). An earlier translation is available at in Wikisource [www].

Zimmern, Alfred, *The Greek Commonwealth: Politics and Economics in Fifth Century Athens*, 5th ed revised (Oxford University Press: Oxford, 1931)

www.ingramcontent.com/pod-product-compliance
Lightning Source LLC
Chambersburg PA
CBHW041541120626
46551CB00019B/2792